BIG FUN
TO GROW
BOOK

Allan A. Swenson's

BIG FUN TO GROW BOOK

Illustrated by Donna R. Sabaka

David McKay Company, Inc.
New York

Library of Congress Cataloging in Publication Data

Swenson, Allan A
Big fun to grow book.

SUMMARY A vegetable and flower gardening guide
including garden planning, flower and vegetable facts,
and a glossary.
1. Flower gardening—Juvenile literature.
2. Vegetable gardening—Juvenile literature. [1. Flower
gardening. 2. Vegetable gardening. 3. Gardening]
I. Title.
SB406.5.S93   635   76-13298
ISBN 0-679-20371-0

10 9 8 7 6 5 4 3 2 1

MANUFACTURED IN THE UNITED STATES OF AMERICA

To Peter, Drew, Boyd, and Meade,
who help grow our family garden
every year. May others profit from the
things you learned and shared.

PREFACE

You can grow the most beautiful flowers and delicious vegetables right in your own backyard or around your home grounds. All you need to know is in this exciting, illustrated *Big Fun to Grow Book*. I've been growing plants of all types since I was your age. I won my first 4-H club gardening prize when I was 10 years old and have enjoyed growing things ever since.

In this book, you'll learn about soil and how to fertilize plants to make them grow bigger, stronger, and more abundant. You'll learn how to encourage helpful insects and do away with harmful ones so they don't bug you or your plants. You'll discover many other good gardening secrets.

You'll also discover how to arrange flowers, plant a window box, create blooming beds and borders. What's more, you'll know when to pick vegetables so they are the tastiest, plumpest, and best for eating and cooking. You'll also find interesting recipes for making tomato juice, pickles, popcorn, and other tasty foods.

Gardening is blooming fun with flowers. It is delicious eating when you grow vegetables. As you plant your tiny seeds, water them, fertilize your plants, and learn how to make all things come alive and grow, you'll be amazed at your own growing skills. So, dig into the fun field of good gardening. It's *Big Fun to Grow* with your family and friends. Get your garden started and see for yourself.

Your Good Gardening Friend,

Allan A. Swenson
America's Green Thumb Gardener

CONTENTS

BIG FUN
TO GROW
BOOK

PLANNING
YOUR GARDEN

READ ABOUT YOUR SEEDS

Every seed packet has a wealth of valuable information on it. Few people really read the package instructions to learn what they should know about that particular variety. Do it, and take the first big step to successful gardening. The second step is to save the empty packet after you have planted the seeds. Wrap it in a plastic sandwich bag. Thumbtack it to your row marker. It will be handy there.

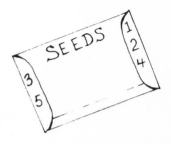

Five basic points:

1. Variety—Each packet tells the variety and gives facts about it such as its size, shape, and the best ways to use the variety.

2. Quantity—You'll find how many plants you can grow or the length of row your seed packet plants.

3. Sowing—You'll find directions as to when, where, and how to sow seeds.

4. Care—Look for special tips to get best results with your variety.

5. Harvesting—Most packets tell when to pick your first crop, what size is best, and when the vegetables are fully ripe. Save the packets so you'll know when the peak of perfection arrives in your garden.

SEEDS ARE FUN TO LEARN ABOUT

There are as many types of seeds as there are plants on our good planet Earth. Some are large, some fuzzy, others round or tiny or armed with barbs.

Now, take a closer look at your seeds. Pick up the larger seeds and carefully take them apart. You may need a pair of tweezers and a small knife. Be very careful when you cut the seeds apart. It helps if you soak the seeds for an hour or two first.

Can you identify the hull or seed coat? This part protects the inner parts of the seeds.

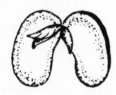

Can you identify the endosperm? That's the food-storage area of the seed which nourishes the plants as they first sprout and begin to grow.

Can you find the germ? That's the part of the seed that actually "sprouts" to begin forming roots, stem, and eventually, as the plant grows, gives rise to all the parts of your happily living new plant.

START EARLY INDOORS

Many places in our country have short summer seasons. If you plant seeds outdoors too early, a late frost may kill the tender seedlings. Luckily, you can stretch the growing season and enjoy more blooming fun if you start seedlings indoors. By doing this you can have sturdy and healthy transplants growing well on your window

4

sill, just waiting for the right time to be placed outside. It's fun and easy when you know how.

Plant seeds indoors about six weeks before the last spring frost in your area. Check with your local garden store. All you need is simple containers. Milk cartons cut in half fit on sunny window sills. Old jars, cans, plastic pots, or whatever will hold soil mix can be used as well. Don't use garden soil. It may contain harmful diseases that kill seedlings. Instead, use prepared seed-starting mix or make your own.

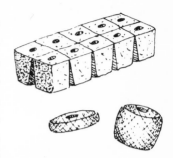

Combine one part peat moss, one part sand (not salty beach sand), and one part vermiculite. Fill the containers with this mix. Be sure there are drainage holes to let excess water escape. Seedlings can't stand wet feet. Peat trays, cubes, and pots are even better for starting seeds indoors. They don't cost much. They do have worthwhile advantages. Seedlings grow quickly in them.

After the last danger of spring frost in your area, simply dig holes, plant pots with individual seedlings in them, and cover with soil. Roots grow right through the peat pot walls. Because you avoid damage to tiny seedling roots, plants get a faster, stronger, better roothold outdoors.

DOUBLE POTTING

Here's a simple, practical way to give your plants a better growing environment. Try double potting. Overwatering is probably the most common cause of failure with house plants and outdoor potted ones, too. Many people kill their plants with misplaced kindness. Too much water rots roots. Leaves turn yellow. Then people add more water, thinking their plant needs it.

Double potting helps avoid overwatering by providing water with a way to escape. Simply plant your seeds or seedlings in a clay pot, putting gravel in the bottom first. Then place this pot inside a larger pot or decorative container. Fill the space between the inner clay pot and outer one with peat or sphagnum moss or with material like vermiculite. This will let excess water and fertilizer seep out through the porous sides of the inner clay pot so that they don't harm the tender plant roots. By double potting you can also use up some of your old chipped or less attractive pots. In this way, nicer-looking containers will hide the inner ones.

This helpful potted-plant culture method is ideal for hanging plants. The extra water that escapes into the outer pot provides the humidity that plants enjoy while protecting them against overwatering.

PICK THE RIGHT SITE

All plants need three ingredients for healthy growth. They need sun, proper nourishment, and enough to drink. The first step is to carefully select the right location. Pick an open spot that gives your plants a sky full of sun, six or more hours each day. Avoid areas near trees. Their roots can rob your plants of light, food, and water. Plan rows running north and south so all plants get the same amount of sun. On sloping land, plant rows across the slope to prevent soil erosion.

BASIC GARDEN TOOLS

Only a few tools are really needed to garden well. You'll want a spade to turn the soil; a rake to smooth out lumps, remove small rocks, and cover seeds. A hoe is handy for planting, weeding, and cultivating. A yardstick helps you space rows the proper distance apart, and sow seeds or set plants their proper distance from each other in the rows. A ball of string and several planting stakes help you mark your rows and keep them even as you plant. You might want a small hand trowel for planting and transplanting. A hand cultivator also can be useful for close-in work around small plants. These tools are easy to find and inexpensive.

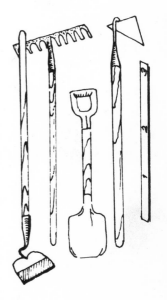

PREPARE YOUR GARDEN

When you feel those first warm days of spring, that's when green thumbs really begin to itch. You'll be tempted to start your garden, but remember that a late frost can kill your tender seedlings. Avoid temptation. Wait until the ground is warm and the soil has dried. Here's a simple test. Pick up a handful of soil. Make a fist. Then open your hand. If the soil crumbles easily, it is ready to be tilled or dug. Hopefully, a friend can turn your soil by rotary tiller. That saves work. If not, dig in with your trusty

spade. Press it into the ground with your feet. Then turn the spadeful 8 inches deep, and continue until the area is completed.

Before digging, some gardeners like to spread lime and fertilizer on the ground to put nutrients down so that plant roots will get them later. If you do, you'll need about 3 pounds of 5-10-5 garden fertilizer per 9 x 12 foot area. Use half that amount for half the garden space. Next, break up big soil clumps with the rake. Then smooth soil well. Mark your measured rows with string between planting stakes, and that's all it takes. You're ready to plant. Careful preparation before you plant will be well worth it when you begin to harvest. Your hard work will show.

SOIL IS ALIVE

Thousands of helpful soil bacteria, microorganisms, and other tiny unseen creatures are at work in the soil. Their important job is to digest and break down old organic matter and minerals into the humus which makes fertile topsoil, layer A. Beneath the topsoil is subsoil, layer B in the chart. Roots must grow into this layer, too. Below this is the parent material of gravel and rock, layer C. You can learn to care for your underground allies, and they will multiply and help you improve the quality of your garden's soil.

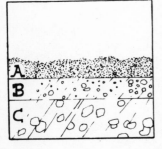

HOW TO IMPROVE IT

Your garden soil may be sandy. It may be sticky clay. Sandy soil dries too fast. Clay soil gets soggy. You can improve both types by adding peat moss and compost. Spread a bale of peat moss 2 inches deep on a 9 x 12 foot area. Then dig it under. You'll notice quickly how the soil condition improves. You can also improve just the immediate area for each plant. Dig a hole and remove the poor soil. Then mix one part peat moss with one part leaf mold or compost and one part soil. Refill the hole with this improved mixture and you'll be ready to plant. Improved soil makes all the difference.

COMPOST IS THE KEY

Let your secret underground allies help you improve your soil. They enjoy all types of organic matter and will digest it into humus. Just build them a compost pile to work in. No soil can have too much organic matter. It improves soil texture. It lets air, water, nutrients, and roots move more freely. Compost also adds nutrients for healthier plant growth.

HOW TO MAKE COMPOST

It's easy to make compost right in your own backyard. Mark off an area about 4 feet square. Pile on old leaves, grass clippings, any plant material—straw, manure, sawdust. Aerobic bacteria like air. If you turn the pile each week these bacteria work faster. Another type, anaerobic, works more slowly. For them, just pile organic material, wet it weekly, and wait. The first method takes a few weeks. The second method takes all season. Either way, you'll get good, rich compost to build better soil.

TRY A PYRAMID GARDEN

Sometimes the soil is so poor with rock and construction debris that it is almost impossible to improve. So try a pyramid garden instead. Measure the area in which you want to grow your garden. Then, ask your parents to build several wooden rectangles of 2 x 6 inch lumber. Make the two top wood rectangles smaller than the bottom. Then, fill the largest one with good topsoil. Place

the medium one on that and fill it, too. Then add the smallest wood frame and fill that. Water the pyramid well. Now you can plant flowers just as the ancients did in the hanging gardens of Babylon or as many people do in parts of the world where land is very scarce and precious. Instead of growing out, you are growing plants up. Be sure to plant the large, deep-rooted plants on top so their roots can grow deeper. With a pyramid, you can enjoy flowers and vegetables provided you water and feed plants as you would in a regular garden.

PLANTING-TIME TIPS

Planting seeds seems simple. But many gardeners don't get started correctly because they don't follow the easy directions on the seed pack. Most people plant seeds too deep. A rule of green thumb is to plant seeds at a depth of only three times the smallest width of the seeds. If the pack says ¼ inch deep, practice a few minutes until you realize how shallow that really is.

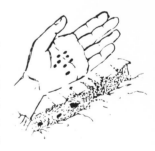

When you have strings strung between row stakes, cut a shallow furrow with your hoe, following the string along the garden row. Just a slit will do for most seeds. Then read the pack again. Sowing too closely wastes seeds. You also make more work for yourself, because you'll need to thin seedlings when they have sprouted so plants aren't too crowded. Wait for a warm day to plant. Cold, damp weather may damage seeds. After sowing, firm soil over seeds with the back of your rake. Tamp gently, but firmly. If soil is dry, sprinkle the garden lightly.

Large seeds, like cucumbers, usually sprout quite well. You can grow these plants in rows, but hill cultivation is usually preferred by expert gardeners. This method saves space since you need only a few hills to provide enough vegetables for an entire family.

Don't make mounds. It may seem funny, but a "hill" is just a circle on the ground. Measure off the space needed for these plants to grow to maturity. Then plant several seeds within the circle or hill. Cover with soil to the right depth.

Firm the soil by tamping it down with your rake or hoe. Then water well. Cucumbers, melons, and squash are all especially thirsty vegetables.

Once seedlings sprout, thin out the weakest, leaving two or three plants per hill. Mulch around this hill periodically to smother weeds.

Seed tape is a new idea. Seeds are inside a soluble tape for easier row planting. When watered, the tape disolves so seeds can sprout. Follow the same rules on planting depth to be sure your seedlings make it to the top, find the sun, and continue to grow. This method is usually foolproof.

MARK GARDEN ROWS

If you save the seed packages, you will be able to thumbtack them on wood stakes to mark your rows. But some people don't think that looks very nice. Well, put your mind to work and design more attractive and useful flower and plant markers. It's easy. There are many ways to do it, too. You can get some tongue depressors from your doctor or school nurse. Coffee-stirring sticks also are good.

Then, trace the picture of your plants on drawing paper or on stiff poster board. You may leave a square or cut a circle. You may also want to cut out the actual design of the blooms. Just thumbtack or staple these to the sticks and neatly mark your rows of seedlings. That way, you'll know what to expect before the flowers bloom. You could also draw pictures or write plant names on the sticks or stakes so you'll always know which varieties are planted where.

TRY INTERPLANTING

You can often get twice the crops from the same garden area if you interplant. Farmers do it. You can plant tall corn and beans so the vines climb the cornstalks. You can plant pumpkins among hills of corn or sunflowers so the vines creep along the ground while the sunflowers or corn grow up. This planting method has advantages.

13

Vine crops, like pumpkins and cukes, shade the ground and act as living mulch. Taller plants do shade the vines, but they usually get enough sun to grow and produce well. Remember when you try interplanting that two types of plants in the same area will need extra water as well as extra plant food. Be sure to give them an extra helping of fertilizer during the growing season, and about half as much again as the normal amount for just one crop in that same growing space.

TRANSPLANT SEEDLINGS

If you started seedlings indoors or perhaps bought some prestarted plants, here's how to help them get the best roothold outdoors.

If possible, pick a cloudy day to transplant outdoors. If soil is dry, moisten the garden an hour before transplanting. Gently remove seedlings from flats, trays, or pots with a little root ball attached. Keep as much of the starter soil on each plant's roots as you can. This avoids root damage. Keep seedlings shielded from hot sun and wind. Dig the hole twice the size of the ball of soil on the plant. Place it in the hole, cover with soil, and firm the soil around the seedling to elimate air pockets. You can plant peat-potted seedlings pot and all.

For most transplanted seedlings, cutworms may be a problem. Make a cardboard collar around the plant that extends 2 inches into the soil and 2 inches above. That usually stops those nasty cutworms cold.

After setting seedlings in their new outdoor spot, sprinkle gently with water. They like it. Within a week, your plants will be sending out new roots. Sprinkle once a week until they get a good start. Then begin adding mulch to smother unwanted weeds that invade your garden. Delicate seedlings can be ruined by weeds.

MULCH AND CULTIVATE

Weeds rob your plants of water, fertilizer, light, and room to grow. They must be controlled—the earlier the better. Mulch is the easiest way. Mulch is any covering of the soil around your plants. It can be black plastic or heavy paper. However, organic mulch—layers of straw, grass clippings, leaves, or compost—is much better. Spread mulch several inches deep around your plants or along the rows. It smothers most tiny weeds and helps hold moisture in the soil. Mulch eventually decays to add small amounts of nutrients to the soil. It also improves the soil's condition, bit by bit.

Mulch early in the season. Add more as the season goes along. Later, just hand-pull weeds that manage to peek through.

If you can't mulch, use your handy hoe. Lightly pull it along the rows to lift out the weeds. Don't dig too deep or you might disturb the plants' roots.

Set aside a special time each week to tend your growing garden. Select one morning, or work after school one day. Take aim on pesky weeds and pull them out, roots and all. Toss them on the compost pile. There

they will be of value soon enough. In compost form weeds are very helpful.

PLANTS NEED FOOD

Plants must eat to stay alive. You must provide food for your plants so they will grow strong and healthy and be productive. Plants get their food from the nutrients that exist in the soil. Their roots absorb dissolved nutrients. Through a process called photosynthesis, with the help of the sun, plants convert their food into new leaves, stems, flowers, fruit, and vegetables. As plants grow, they use up the nutrients in the soil. You must replace the nutrients with fertilizer.

There are three major plant foods that are vital for strong, steady, healthy plant growth. These are nitrogen, phosphorus, and potash. On fertilizer bag labels these are listed as N, P, and K, and always in the same order. Nitrogen is important for building foliage, stems, stalks, and leaves. Phosphorus builds flowers, fruit set, seed, and plant sugars. Potash builds healthy root systems. All three are needed for a balanced plant diet.

When you apply fertilizer, use only the amount suggested on the fertilizer bag label. Too much food can actually hurt plants. They like enough to eat, but not too much. If your plants don't respond, recheck their fertilizer diet. Watch them closely, since fertilizer is an important growth ingredient.

WATER WELL AND WISELY

Flowers won't flourish if they're thirsty, and most vegetables consist mainly of water. That's why water is so important for growing plants successfully. Too much is just as bad as too little. Here are tips for proper watering.

Your garden needs about one inch of water every week. If it rains, fine. If not, you must make up the difference. Remember that roots of plants grow much deeper than you would suspect. It is better to water deeply and less often than just to sprinkle lightly more frequently. Soaker hoses are ideal. They let water seep into the soil slowly. Rotating sprinklers or those that swing back and forth are also useful. Just wetting leaves doesn't do much good. In fact, it only helps surface roots. Deeper watering encourages plants to send roots deeper down to where most plant foods are found.

You can easily measure the water content in your garden. Dig down 8 inches with a spade. If soil is moist there, water is reaching the proper depth. Mulch is especially important in hot, dry areas. Mulch helps reduce evaporation from the soil so the water stays where plant roots can use it as they should. Without mulch covering, tender roots can even become exposed. Dry areas need a heavier mulch than cool areas.

FRIENDLY INSECTS

Certain insects and worms are important inhabitants of your garden.

Ladybugs are tiny flying beetles. They are bright orange with black spots on their wings. Some types are darker. Both adult ladybugs and the larvae that hatch from their eggs have enormous appetites. In one season they'll eat tens of thousands of aphids and other harmful insects.

The praying mantis looks ferocious. However, it won't harm you, though its appetite for nasty pests is tremendous.

You can buy ladybug and praying mantis egg cases from garden catalogs. When they arrive, simply place them around your yard as directed.

Earthworms are helpful. They eat organic matter in the soil as they tunnel through it on their daily rounds. This helps in two ways: First, they leave behind castings—the digested organic material from their eating. Second, worm burrows let air, water, and plant nutrients move more freely in your garden soil. This helps improve it.

As you add organic matter to your garden soil, you encourage more worms. The more the merrier, so they continue improving soil to help plants grow more abundantly. Improved soil makes plants flourish.

CAUTIONS ABOUT PESTICIDES

Farmers have needed to control harmful pests for years. Otherwise, the pests would have eaten their crops. Scientists have developed different types of pesticides. These are the chemicals that kill insects. Since they kill insects, pesticides can be harmful to people, too. Every label on pesticide containers has a warning. Before anyone, including parents and other adults, uses a pesticide spray or dust, he or she should read the label carefully.

Then remember these extra warnings: Never use pesticides by yourself. Always ask for an adult's supervision for any chemical control of pests. In small home gardens, if you check every week and hand-pick insect and worm enemies, there will be few times that pesticides will be needed. Never get pesticides on your skin, and always wash carefully if you have been exposed to pesticide sprays. Never open any pesticide containers without permission. After chemicals have been used, always check to see that containers are put away. Better yet, make sure they are locked away safely from any younger friends. Remember, pesticides are poisons and can harm people if not used properly.

BIRDS CONTROL BUGS

Birds can be wonderful friends in your flower garden and in vegetable gardens, too. After all, they sing nicely. More important, birds eat bugs. If you encourage birds to visit your garden regularly, they will devour thousands of bugs, ants, plant lice, and other pests. Put up some birdhouses. Place a birdbath in the garden and keep it filled with clean, fresh water. Put bits of string on branches of shrubs so the birds can build nests. The more you encourage birds, the more they will help you by controlling buggy pests.

Chickadees, nuthatches, and downy woodpeckers eat aphids or plant lice. Purple martins and barn swallows love mosquitoes. Barn swallows also eat chinch bugs and weevils. If you have ant problems, you'll want to attract house wrens, flycatchers, brown creepers, and chickadees. If you have wasps nesting nearby, barn swallows and flycatchers like them. Grasshoppers can be a problem, too. Bluebirds and wrens will eat them. When you buy or make birdhouses, be sure the holes are the right size so that small songbirds aren't evicted by larger, less useful starlings. Bring back birds to your garden and they'll sing for their supper. That surely is a sweet sound to hear.

20

SHED LIGHT ON PLANTS

If you live in an apartment or you don't have a nice, sunny location to plant a garden, cheer up. You still can enjoy gardening all year long. All you need to do is replace our natural sun with an artificial one. You can shed light on plants by using excellent new bulbs and fluorescent tubes that are especially made to duplicate the sun's rays for good plant growth. You can grow the plants in pots or trays—just about anywhere you can plug lights into an electric socket. In fact, just a few lights will be enough to grow many plants all year. These light fixtures are reasonably priced.

You can even buy a special bulb and use it in a regular lamp. These new bulbs are called Dyro Lite Plant Lite or Krypten Plant Lite. All you do is screw one of these bulbs into a light socket and place it over your seedlings or plants.

There are several types of fluorescent bulbs, too; those long types, which have been made to duplicate as closely as possible the sun's beneficial, plant-stimulating rays. One is called Gro Lux. It has a purplish ray that will improve the appearance of your blooms. To use these and other long tube lights, you will need fluorescent fixtures. Some are only 18 inches long. You can also obtain some 3 or 4 feet long, single-, twin-, or four-tube types with reflectors to focus the light rays on your plants. It is best to obtain adjustable fixtures so that you can

21

adjust them as you wish. They should be lower for smaller plants and starting seeds. As plants grow, just raise the lights so the plants can mature properly. Other excellent fluorescent lights are called Dura Test Naturescent and Optima. Both provide good, bright light. And it is more natural to the eye. These don't have the purplish rays, but they do supply the needed plant growth-stimulating light that flowering plants must have.

You can use artificial lights in dark corners or to supplement daylight near windows that don't receive sufficient light for perfect plant growth. The directions for proper use of these new types of artificial lights are included with them. In fact, helpful booklets are usually packed with the light fixtures or available from your supplier. Follow the usual methods for growing plants with proper soil, water, and plant food as you do for plants that get their fair share of sunlight. You'll find that these new inventions can help you garden almost anywhere as well as you could with the sun.

FLOWER FACTS

AMAZING ANNUALS

Some flowers, such as petunias, are known as annuals. You must plant the seeds each year or purchase prestarted plants from garden centers unless you live in an area that is not reached by fall frosts. Frost and freezing weather will kill annual flowers.

Many people prefer annuals because they find that these plants let them have one type of garden one year, and then they can select different annuals for different colors and patterns the next year.

Here are some general rules of good green thumb about annuals. You should start seeds indoors in pots, trays, or tubs 6 to 8 weeks before you want to plant them outside. Always wait until the last killing frost in your area has passed before planting tender annuals outdoors. You can easily find when that is by asking your local garden center or gardening friends who have lived in your area for several years.

Some annuals prefer sun. Others like a bit of shade. Some like it hot and dry. Others thrive only when the weather is cool and moist.

Seed catalogs and the back of seed packets provide a wealth of additional information about the best location of various flowers. You'll learn the height to which individual plants mature. That's important. When you know how tall your annuals will grow, you can plan to plant taller ones to the rear of beds so they can reach their most striking beauty without shading or crowding lower-growing neighbors or blocking your view of the other annuals in the bed.

Here is a list of some popular annual flowers and the conditions they prefer. When you provide the right conditions they'll reward you with happier and more colorful displays.

For light shade try asters, balsam, cleome, cornflowers, impatiens, larkspur, lupine, and nicotiana. Also pansies, salvia, snapdragons, sweet alyssum, vinca, and violas.

For sunny, drier areas try California poppies, calliopsis, cosmos, and four-o'clocks. Also petunias, phlox, portulaca, salvia, verbena, and zinnias.

TRY PERENNIALS FROM SEED

The joy of perennials is not just their blooming beauty, but the fact that once you plant them, they reward you year after year. With annuals, you must replant them each spring. Perennials become part of your permanent landscape.

Many perennials are available as started plants. For economy you can start many from seeds and grow your own plants. For the same amount of money you can enjoy a much wider range of flowers.

The following are perennials that may be grown from seed: achillea, alyssum, anemones, asters, candytuft, carnations, Chinese lantern, chrysanthemums, columbine, coral bell, coreopsis, and Shasta daisy. Also day lily, delphiniums, dianthus, forget-me-nots, cloriosa daisy, hollyhock, lavender, lilies of different types, linum, lupine, polyanthus, poppies, scabiosa, trumpet vine, verbena, venosa, and violas.

There are lots more, of course. Some are more difficult to grow than others. But with patience and tender loving care, you'll find that you can create a more beautiful home and garden with perennials. As you do, you will find them popping up each year to add their beauty and their fragrance to your blooming world.

WHICH PLANTS SHOULD BE PLANTED WHERE?

That's a question many people ask. After all, there are so many types, colors, shapes, and sizes of flowers and just as many places to grow them that we can all become confused at times. Here are some guidelines. They are only general suggestions based on the type of soil, sun, moisture, and other conditions that suit these particular plants best.

For window boxes try alyssum, begonias, coleus, geraniums, ivy, lobelia, marigolds, petunias, verbena, and vinca.

For low beds and edging try ageratum, alyssum, English daisy, lobelia, dwarf marigold, pansies, portulaca, violas, and dwarf zinnias.

For rock gardens try ageratum, alyssum, asters, aubrieta, California poppies, candytuft, dianthus, forget-me-nots, lobelia, phlox, portulaca, verbena, and dwarf zinnias.

For hanging baskets try begonias, lobelia, nasturtiums, petunias, and Thunbergia. Of course, you can use a wide range of typical house plants, too.

For moist areas try caladiums, ferns, forget-me-nots, foxglove, impatiens, lily of the valley, polyanthus, sweet violets, vinca, and violas.

A NOSE FOR FRAGRANCE

Some flowers reward you with their beautiful blooms. Others have the added attraction of their unusual foliage. Some combine both blooms and foliage for striking displays. Many, unfortunately, are lovely to look at, but just don't seem to have the delicate fragrances of flowers grown back in the good old days. Luckily, some still do retain the sweet aromas and heady fragrances of old-fashioned flowers.

As a general rule, standard varieties have more fragrance than new hybrids. In the process of creating new hybrids, sometimes the sweet smell of success of growing bigger, more colorful, and longer-lasting blooms has become more important than the sweet smell of the blooms themselves. However, if you are looking for fragrance, here are some flowers you should consider for your garden: alyssum, carnation, heliotrope, lavender, lilies and lily of the valley, mock orange, nicotiana, peony, petunias, phlox, stock, and sweet pea. You might also select tuberose, wallflower, and wisteria for the aromas they cast out upon the breeze.

Of course, some new varieties among the hybrids do retain the fragrances of their parent stock. As you explore the world of flowers, your nose will soon tell you which ones are the best.

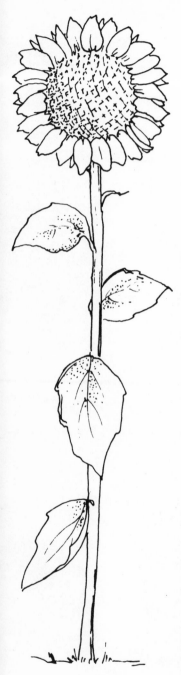

SUPER
SUNFLOWERS

The earliest pioneers who crossed our great prairies years ago found millions of bright sunflowers stretching out before them, mile after mile. As they discovered the value of these plants for food and livestock feed, they realized that sunflowers are not only lovely, but are a practical plant for the garden. Today, Kansas honors the sunflower as its state flower and is called the Sunflower State.

Since those early days, many improvements have been made from the native flowers. You can grow smaller, bushy types for colorful displays. Or, for fun and good eating, you can cultivate the tallest and truly gigantic ones that seem to keep climbing right to the sky. All sunflowers aren't the typical bright-yellow-leaved type. Some have wine red or chestnut hue in their petals. Sunflowers are quite hardy. They grow well in most soil conditions, but as their name says, sunflowers enjoy and must have lots of strong sunshine to really thrive.

You can challenge your friends to a super sunflower growing contest to see who can grow the biggest, the tallest, or the heaviest-headed one. It's lots of fun in the sun with super sunflowers.

SUNFLOWER HISTORY

Like marigolds, zinnias, and other popular flowers, sunflowers are native to America. They are members of the Compositae family. The scientific name for sunflowers is *Helianthus annuus*. When the early explorer Champlain visited Indians near Lake Huron, he found them busy cultivating the large, common sunflowers which had been brought by the traveling tribes from their original home on the great prairies. Indians and early pioneers grew the sunflowers for the fibers of the stalks and made livestock feed from the leaves. They valued the seeds for food and oil. Settlers also sent seeds to their homelands, where the plants grew well.

Today, sunflowers are also widely grown in Russia, China, India, Egypt, Peru, and Chile. The seeds are so rich in fat and protein that they are used widely as livestock feed. In many parts of our world, sunflower seeds are roasted and eaten like peanuts. In fact, as more people have discovered the value of natural foods, sunflowers have gained wider popularity. One of the unusual habits of this fun plant is an ability to turn its flowers to follow the sun. That, most likely, is why it was named sunflower by the earliest American pioneers.

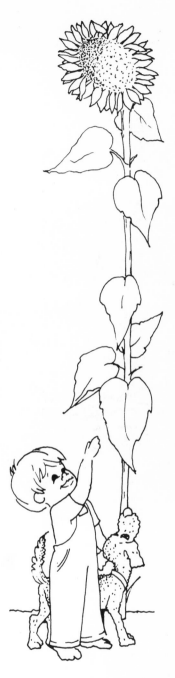

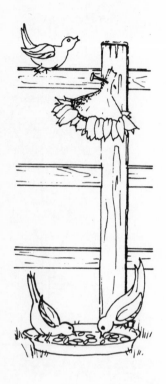

TRY OTHER VARIETIES

Sunflowers are for the birds. That's what most people think. It's true enough because birds love sunflower seeds. You can watch them feasting for hours on the large, meaty seeds. Sunflowers are for people, too. They give us blooms larger than most any other plants. That makes them fun to watch as they soar from tiny seeds to 20-foot-tall plants with bursting golden heads bigger than our own. Their seeds are good to eat, too. People in health food stores know that. You can try several varieties for show and some for show and tell as well. There are types that grow so big they will amaze all your friends. The smaller varieties are beautiful plants for use as screens or backgrounds. They're hardy, too, and will thrive in any soil that gets full sun 8 hours each day. One smaller sunflower with double yellow blooms grows on bushy plants only 2 feet tall. Its name is Teddy Bear. A relative called Sungold is taller. It grows almost 5 feet high and has double golden yellow flowers, too. They are a bit more showy. Old Red is even bigger. It bears its shaded chestnut red blooms some 6 feet above the ground. Often this variety has petals tipped with yellow or a blend of red and yellow.

Your real big fun begins when you plant those super-tall sunflowers. Giant Russian and Mammoth start from seeds that you don't think could ever grow into plants as high as a one-story house. But grow they do.

Just plant the seeds and water well. Give them a sprinkle every day for about 14 days until they sprout and take their stand. Then for fun, keep a record of their growth. You'll be amazed how much these plants do grow each week. All sunflowers need lots of full sun. That's how they got their name. Mammoth, the big tall one, grows so high you'll need a stepladder to reach its head to pick the seeds. This type and its relatives yield full heads of plump striped seeds aplenty. Each is well filled with meat. Song-birds and poultry, too, enjoy the seeds. Later on you'll find a recipe so that you, too, can enjoy sunflower seeds. When you plant these largest sunflowers, remember that they need lots of room and lots to drink. Any plant that grows so tall and sets so many seeds does. This year, enjoy super sunflowers.

FUN WITH SUNFLOWERS

You can grow flowers high in the sky when you grow sunflowers. These marvels of nature are super large these days, thanks to efforts of plant breeders who developed taller plants with bigger, sunnier heads and lots more seeds for you and your feathered friends to eat. As long as you have a spot with full sun all day, you can grow these giants. Try some beneath your bedroom window, even if it is on the second floor of your house. Plant a few seeds, water them well, and add a cup of plant food around the group when they are about 3 to 4 feet tall. Add another cupful when they are 8 to 10 feet high. Water after you apply the fertilizer. That extra plant food can boost their growth so that their heads will be shining in your window when they are fully grown. Then, just watch them get plump and ripe and ready to pick and eat.

If you have a dog that sleeps in a little kennel outdoors, perhaps sunflowers will give him a bit of shade during the summer's heat. Plant medium or tall varieties to provide enough shade. Sunflowers belong in other places, too. They are fine to hide trash cans or an ugly garage wall. In fact, they grow so quickly that they make a blooming fence to divide a play area from other parts of your home grounds. Think where they will do best around your yard. How about a living hideout for your games? Sunflowers and pole beans grow naturally together. You simply sow the sunflowers and let them grow to several feet tall. Then, plant some pole beans in a circle around them. When your beans are sending out their growing tips, put them right in touch with the stalks of your sunflowers. Just a few bean plants are enough. As beans grow round and round, your sunflowers keep growing taller. In weeks they'll reach full height. By then the beans will have circled right up the stalks. You can play hide-and-seek, take a nap, or just enjoy watching your flowers and beans grow taller day by day. Before fall frost, pick the rest of your beans. Then pick the sunflower seeds or cut off the heads. If you cut them, keep them in a cool, dry place so seeds won't start to mold. Better yet, remove the seeds and spread them on some boards in the sun to dry out well. Try sunflowers wherever you have lots of sun. They're a fun plant to brighten any garden.

SUNFLOWER SEEDS

Sunflower seeds are delicious and nutritious, too. Many people around the world have learned that these seeds are rich in protein. You, too, can enjoy them. All you need are some cookie baking trays and help from your parents. Pick the seeds from the mature sunflower heads. Dry them in the sun a few days first or spread them on the cookie sheets indoors at a sunny window. Then, sprinkle vegetable cooking oil lightly on the seeds. Next, sprinkle on some salt, about the same amount you would enjoy on buttered popcorn. Then bake the sunflower seeds in a slow oven, heated to 300°F. You should, of course, always ask for help before you use an oven. Bake the seeds until they seem fully dried. It may take you a few tries to tell when seeds are done. Then, split a few and add more salt to the seed "meat" you pick from the shells. Add more salt to taste. Once you try them, you'll probably want to grow more next year.

MARVELOUS
MARIGOLDS

Marigolds are as American as apple pie. These beautiful flowers, which are native to the Americas, are among the easiest annuals you can grow. Originally there were only a few varieties. Today, thanks to the dedicated efforts of plant breeders, you can enjoy a wide and colorful choice of marigolds. They grow well in beds and borders, and bloom profusely in pots or even in lovely hanging baskets for windows and patios. You can select from the many yellow, orange, and even reddish-colored marigolds. Now you can even grow a pure white one.

The search for a pure white marigold was launched many years ago by Mr. David Burpee, president of the W. Atlee Burpee Company. Year by year, he and his staff tried crossbreeding the best and nearest-to-white marigolds. To enlist others in the search, David Burpee even offered a $10,000 reward to the first person who could discover or grow a pure white marigold. Finally, in 1975, a lady discovered white blooms on a plant in her garden. Seeds from that plant grew new plants bearing white blooms, earning her $10,000. Although the prize money has been won, you can still enjoy great fun with rainbows of marvelous marigolds.

MARIGOLD HISTORY

The marigold is really a native of the Americas. When the Spanish explorer Cortez conquered ancient Mexico, he discovered marigolds growing in many of the gardens there. They were so beautiful that he took seeds with him back to Spain. There, too, they quickly became popular. The fact is, these lovely marigolds became such favorites of the devout that they were often placed at the altar of the Virgin Mary. That's how they received their name, "Mary's Gold," which later became simply "Marigold." Marigolds are so easily grown in all parts of the world that you can find them in gardens around the globe.

Although the smallest marigolds are called French marigolds and the tall types often called African marigolds, the fact

remains that these lovely flowers are really American. In India, the marigold has become the favorite flower for making leis to place around a person's neck as a sign of friendship, earning it the name "Friendship Flower." Since marigolds grow well in every state and are symbols of friendship, it is the dream of famed horticulturist David Burpee that one day the marigold may win its ultimate tribute—to be named America's national flower. You see, there is none now.

VARIETIES FOR GARDENS

From gold and yellow to bronze and orange, from reddish to pure white, you can pick your pleasure from the carefree flower world of marigolds. They are easily grown in any state.

GIANT CHRYSANTHEMUM TYPES

Tallest of the marigold family, the giant marigolds bear flowers several inches wide. They provide nice, tall backgrounds for low-growing plants. Fantastic Orange has flared, curled petals and graceful dark-green foliage on sturdy 3-foot-tall stalks. Giant Fluffy marigolds offer several different colors and 4-inch blooms.

CARNATION-FLOWERED TYPES

Another recent relative, the Hybrid marigold, bears blooms several inches wide on 24-inch-tall plants. Often 50 or more blooms may open at the same time. First Lady is an All-America winner, with lovely light-yellow flowers all season. Gold Lady has masses of golden blooms, while Orange Lady shows orange blooms.

CLIMAX MARIGOLDS

These biggest-flowered marigolds may bear blooms 5 inches or more across. They're well ruffled for beautiful arrangements. Golden, Yellow, and Primrose Climax all grow at least 2 feet tall. Toreador is a deep-orange All-America award winner.

HEDGE-TYPE MARIGOLDS

These grow so uniformly that they are usually grown as hedges. All mature about 2 feet high with fine flowers 4 inches wide. Try Diamond Jubilee for bright yellow, and Golden or Orange Jubilee for their respective colors.

FRENCH MARIGOLDS

These attractive, low-growing marigolds bloom all summer and right up to frost.

They fit well in beds, borders, and as potted plants. French marigolds offer more shades of orange and red than other types. Fireglow has bright mahogany-scarlet markings mixed with gold. King Tut has double-type flowers, reddish with yellow.

Short or tall, plain or fancy, marigolds provide colorful pleasure aplenty.

MIX MARIGOLDS AND VEGETABLES

Flowers can add beauty to your vegetable garden. They make other contributions, too. Marigolds are known to control nasty nematodes, those harmful tiny worms that damage vegetable roots. Marigolds also help chase rabbits away from cabbages and beans. In fact, many organic gardeners use marigolds in their vegetable gardens to discourage a variety of insect pests. Perhaps it is the odor of the foliage that works. The fact remains, marigolds have extra value beyond their beauty. That alone is good reason to interplant these fine flowers with vegetables.

They'll add perfume and beauty to your outdoor living room while you grow food, as well. Try marigolds among lettuce, or around tomatoes. You can use the tall types as colorful accents against darker-green vegetable foliage. Try dwarf marigolds among lower vegetables.

GROW
GREAT
ZINNIAS

Zinnias are one of the most popular annual flowers grown in our country. No wonder. They are easily started from seed, are hardy even if grown in somewhat poor and sandy soil, and provide a wide range of sizes and colors in the garden. In addition, zinnias offer long-lasting blooms as cut flowers. During recent years, plant breeders have continued to improve zinnias. Today, many hybrid types grow faster, taller, and brighter with bigger blooms. Just as important are the strikingly different petal and flower forms—from ruffled ones that look almost like chrysanthemums to those with ball-shaped blooms that add sparkle to floral arrangements. The hardy habit of zinnias lets you grow them in beds and borders, and among vegetables, too. The smaller types are perfect for window boxes and in potted plants on balconies or patios. In recent years, even more attention has been focused on zinnias. This is because many zinnia varieties grow tall, creating a sturdy hedge effect to set off many lower-growing flowers, including the smaller types of zin-

nias. In fact, you can select many All-America winners for an All-America zinnia garden to grow the best and biggest blooms in town. They are great for flower shows, too.

ZINNIA HISTORY

Zinnias are members of the Compositae family. Like marigolds, zinnias are also native to the New World. The first zinnias were discovered long ago by the earliest explorers of Mexico. Later expeditions into the southwestern part of the United States and as far down as the coast of Chile in the southernmost tip of South America also found zinnias growing wild in the hot, dry, and usually sandier soils which are typical of these areas. Seeds of zinnias were taken back to Europe, but the flower did not gain the same immediate wide popularity that the marigold did. Probably the fact that marigolds grow well under much wider growing conditions led to their greater popularity. However, zinnias have attracted continued attention from plant breeders, who have worked for years to develop a

broad range of new colors, shapes, and sizes, as well as hardier hybrids that perform with outstanding success in most gardens. Zinnias are classed as a tender annual or perennial herb, according to botanists. Today, thanks to the art of dedicated plant breeders, you have a wonderfully colorful world of many types of zinnias for beds and borders, for window boxes, and even as hanging basket decorations for your home.

VARIETIES FOR GARDENS

There are tiny Lilliput zinnias of many different colors. Some are red and yellow; others are white and gold and orange. You can grow multicolor zinnias of many shapes and sizes. If you like giant flowers, then the super Jumbo zinnias with blossoms 7 inches wide let you do your blooming thing. These zany zinnias grow fast and well all across America. They are one of our most popular annuals.

JUMBO ZINNIAS

Jumbos are really big. Their blooms are ruffled. When plants are 18 inches tall, the blooms are 5 to 6 inches across. They seem to radiate a glow. Plants are mature when they reach 30 inches. Scarlet has a rich, red hue. Others range from white to pink, with salmon, rose, and orange shades for you to enjoy all season.

GIANT-FLOWERED ZINNIAS

You might think these are the biggest and they were—until the Jumbos were developed. Still, Giants have showy blooms up to 5 inches wide on strong, branching plants. Canary Bird is, of course, yellow. Dream is lavender. Exquisite is rose with a red center. Salmon, white, scarlet, and mixed provide as wide a range of colors as you can wish to have with zinnias.

BICOLOR ZINNIAS

These lovely plants have blooms that seem almost to change from day to day. Flowers have stripes and wedges of red and white, or yellow and orange. The plants are bushy and 18 inches tall, with blooms several inches across.

HYBRID ZENITH ZINNIAS

Some zinnias have been created to give more flowers and to have longer periods of blooming. Zenith zinnias are bushier than others and offer as wide a choice of colors. Bonanza is rich gold-orange. Firecracker is rich red. Rosy Future is rose-pink. You can enjoy crimson, orange, yellow, or white Zenith zinnias, getting dozens of 5- to 6-inch blooms all season long to frost.

POMPON OR LILLIPUT ZINNIAS

These are the smallest of the zinnia family. Plants are dwarf and bushy. They grow only 12 to 18 inches high, but are covered with many 1- to 2-inch blooms from early summer until frost. Canary Gem is rich yellow, while Crimson is rich red. Pink or scarlet, white or rose, these low-growing zinnias are excellent for every garden, especially in beds. Of course, there are other types of zinnias. You can try Mexicana zinnias, or Mini zinnias that are only 6 inches tall. There are hybrid Peter Pan and Thumbelina types, too. Whichever you select, zinnias can really sparkle.

FUN WITH ZINNIAS

Fortunately, zinnias are available in tall, medium, and short varieties, so you can plan a complete zinnia garden all in one area. Dig the soil well. Then, plan your zinnia display on paper. Map out where the tallest, medium, and tiniest should be. Those low-growing ones should be on the southern side so the taller ones do not shade them too much. Next, map your rows. Then plant. As they grow, the darker foliage of the tallest will provide a background for the lower blooms of the medium and small zinnias. You can, of course, plant other lower-growing flowers like allysum or dwarf marigolds in front. It's up to you. The main thing to remember is that by picking varieties that mature to different heights, you can have an appealing and dazzling display when you mix and match different varieties in one beautiful bed or border.

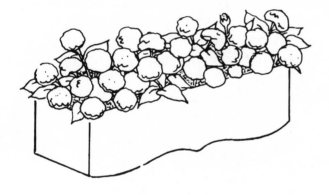

THE
AMERICAN
ASTER

Asters are as American as apple pie, too. Actually, some types have been developed from parent stock found in other parts of the world. The fact remains that most of today's lovely asters trace their heritage to North America, which claims some 250-plus species in the wild across the continent.

Although you are only somewhat limited in choice of colors, asters make up for this lack in other ways. They are excellent for beds and your blooming borders. The lower-growing varieties provide profusions of blooms as living bouquets. They are also ideal for use in pots or planters on porch or patio.

The taller-growing types lend themselves to background planting in your flower garden. Being tall and strong-stemmed, they also are fine for cuttings and are long-lasting as cut flowers.

Some asters bloom early. Others begin blooming in mid season, while others are fine for grand color right up to fall frost. You can also use these popular annuals for window sill and box gardens.

The perennial asters, with their large flowers but short plant growth, do well in rock gardens and borders. As perennials, once you have them well established, they will appear early each spring to give you color in May and June, and even earlier in southern regions.

ASTER HISTORY

Asters earned their name from the distinctive starlike way they bloom. If you look closely at wild or cultivated asters, you'll see they all have the typical radiating or starlike flower head. It may vary from a half-inch among some smaller wild species to several bursting, highly colorful inches in the newer varieties seen in many home gardens. "Aster" comes from the Greek word *aster*, which means simply "star."

Asters belong in the same family as marigolds and daisies and that all-too-frequent pest of lawns, the common dandelion. The family name is Compositae. Many species of wild asters still grace the woods, fields, roadsides, and even deserts of the Americas.

According to botanists, there are more than 250 different species of asters on this continent. Most wild asters are perennial plants. Some of the best cultivated types are, too.

Thanks to plant breeders your garden can be a mass of white and blue and red and pink asters in lovely shades and many sizes. Most cultivated asters are considered annuals rather than perennials, since they can be killed by hard frosts and winters.

Typical of asters, in addition to their starlike blooming pattern, are the rough stems and leaves. Despite a lack of lovely foliage, these blooming friends deserve a place in your home garden.

COLORFUL ASTER VARIETIES

Asters offer a profusion of blooms for gardens everywehere. The following varieties are hardy from summer right into the fall.

EARLY ASTERS

These asters in blue, rose, red, and white offer the advantage of really early bloom. They are wilt-resistant and erect, maturing to about 20 to 24 inches tall. They bloom several weeks earlier than most others. Flowers are globular and double with blooms 3 to 4 inches across with curved petals.

For blue, try Blue Boy, a striking dark blue. Blue Sky is a lavender blue. Rose is a bright one with salmon tint. Scarlet Morn is a rich crimson scarlet, while Snow Ball is glistening white.

Some asters are not quite so early, but have bushy spreading growth and bear to late summer. Red is carmine-colored. White has bright, pure white and Blue is a rich mid-blue. Azure Blue is a clear azure color. All mature about 18 inches tall.

TOTEM POLE ASTERS

This type offers a bouquet blooming growth habit. Plants grow 8 to 10 inches long, and have strong stems with giant, shaggy, double flowers 6 to 7 inches across. They are good for cuttings.

With these you can also go patriotic with Scarlet Cerise, White and Azure, or Dark Blue. For somewhat smaller blooms on taller plants, try Scarlet Beauty, White Beauty, or Blue Beauty Asters.

FLUFFY ASTERS

This aster has large flowers 4 to 5 inches across with distinctive fluffy form. Petals curl like ostrich plumes. They mature about 18 inches tall. You can enjoy red, white, pink, or blue, or mix all for a dazzling display.

DWARF ASTERS

If you prefer the shorter types for beds, pots, window boxes, or your low-growing plant borders, the dwarf branching asters will be more appropriate for you. There are red or rose, white, and blue varieties for your gardens.

DWARF BORDER ASTERS

Dwarf border asters are compact, only growing 10 inches tall. They spread well up to 18 inches and have a profusion of blooms. Red, white, and blue are the colors.

POMPON ASTERS

These smallest-flowered asters have nicely rounded blooms, about 2 inches across. Colors range from white, pink, carmine, and crimson to blue and violet.

TRY A PATRIOTIC BUNTING

Asters have a limited color range. They are mainly red, white, and blue, with shades of these basic colors including pink, rose, violet, and lavender.

Since they are native to America it seems natural they should provide our country's colors for distinctive patriotic gardens. Here's how to plant a living bunting of red, white, and blue rosettes.

Prepare your garden soil well, as you would for any flowers. Since asters enjoy sunlight, give them a prime location for showy display.

Mark the rows with stakes. For rosettes, use alternate circles of lime and bare earth so you can plant red, white, and blue plants just where they belong.

Dwarf asters and border asters are best

for these gardens. Here are good choices. For red, try Scarlet, a deep scarlet color. For white, plant Snow White, which is a glistening, bright white.

For blue you have a choice of Blue, which is a good mid-blue, or Deep Blue, which is really a violet blue.

Since these dwarf, compact asters only grow 10 inches high but spread to about 18 inches, allow them growing room. Mulch with peat moss to prevent weeds until they begin to expand. They'll fill in nicely and provide a bountiful display to help you celebrate your American heritage with living cascades of color.

THE
POPULAR
PETUNIA

Petunias have become more and more popular each year. For many, they once seemed difficult to start because they have such tiny seeds. However, the new, hardier hybrid varieties that have been developed have helped petunias really gain ground in popularity. You can also buy them quite inexpensively as started plants at garden centers everywhere.

From the simple single-flowered types of long ago, plant breeders have developed double- and nearly triple-flowered types in wide assortments of striking colors and multicolors.

Petunias will grow almost anywhere they can have good soil, warm sun, and sufficient room to bloom happily. Some grow almost 2 feet tall. Most, however, are more low-growing, 8 to 12 inches. The compact types do best in beds and borders.

For hanging baskets and profuse blooms all season, you can enjoy the well-named cascading type. You can mix petunias with other flowers for beautiful effects.

Petunias are one of the more versatile flowers. They can't take frost, which kills them, but with protection on fall nights, you can keep petunias blooming many weeks longer than most people realize.

PETUNIA HISTORY

A native of South America, as so many popular flowers are, the petunia has been cultivated since the early 19th century in many gardens around the world. It was originally found in Argentina and Brazil in its plainer, single-flowered form.

The original petunias belong to the same family as the potato and nightshade, Solanaceae. As flowers, they showed promise of responding to the creative talents of plant breeders. Today, the profusions of petunia blooms across America are a tribute to the work of dedicated plant scientists. Most modern hybrids are usually of *Petunia nyctaginiflora* and *Petunia violaceae* ancestry.

From the simple original petunias you now have a choice of brilliantly colored varieties in the full range of the rainbow. In addition, you can enjoy the fluted and fringed as well as multicolored and double-flowered types.

Depending on where and how you choose to use petunias, you can plant cascading types or more upright ones. Because many varieties tend to sag and sprawl, you can use that seeming disadvantage to have them cover banks, stone walls, or fill an empty area with glowing color.

For beds and borders, you can select the special dwarf and compact strains. These, too, bear well, but won't overgrow their surroundings.

PETUNIA VARIETIES

Pick any color you like. Your choice is wide and brilliant when you grow petunias. They range from bright white to dark purple, rose, red, yellow, and pink in many hues, from vivid to pastel. Here are some different types to add to your fun.

GRANDIFLORAS

These have superb well-waved, large blooms with clear, bright colors. This type is earlier and more free-flowering for bedding, pots, and window boxes.

Try Blue Lace with medium-size well-fringed, light orchid-blue blooms that have deep violet-blue veins. Blue Magic is a deep velvety violet. Mariner is violet blue and compact.

Matado has large crimson flowers and grows 14 inches tall. Bravo is bright red with a golden throat. It is compact in growth. El Toro is hot red. Red Cascade is fiery red and flows well for hanging baskets.

For pink, try Chiffon Cascade for boxes and baskets. It is pastel pink with a creamy throat. Flamboyant opens rich red, then changes to reddish pink. Pink Cascade has huge blooms of carmine pink. Pink Snow is light pink with wavy blooms.

Among bicolors try Astro, a rich scarlet red with white bars—a popular variety. Fandango is deep violet-blue with white. It does well in hanging displays. Sabre Dance bears huge blooms of rich crimson and white in free-flowering beauty.

MULTIFLORA PETUNIAS

These free-flowering hybrids have vivid colors. For white try White Satin or Polar Cap. Yellow Gleam is vigorous with lemon-yellow color.

Sparkles is reddish rose. Coral Satin is deep salmon, and Orange Bells rings orange-scarlet. Purple Plum and Purple Satin both are nice.

Among bicolors Glitters Improved is rosy red and white. Star Joy has super-rich carnation rose blooms, defined by a white star.

GIANT DOUBLES

These petunias offer giant flowers, double fringed. Most grow about 1 foot tall. For blues, try Blue Danube with its lovely lavender blue marked by violet veins. Allegro is bright salmon, but opens scarlet. Circus is an All-America winner with deep salmon marked with white. Colossal Shades of Rose is salmon pink to deep carmine.

DOUBLE MULTIFLORA

These exciting petunias offer masses of medium-size blooms, doubled and free-flowering. They are best for bedding or window box displays.

Apple Tart is red. Cherry Tart is rose and white. Peach Tart is soft salmon and Plum Tart is lilac pink with purple veins.

You'll find many other petunia varieties in stores and seed company catalogs. There's a colorful world of them to brighten your garden all season.

CASCADING HANGUPS OF COLOR

Petunias offer you such colorful displays it is difficult to select the varieties you like most. But for hanging baskets, your choice is made easier. The cascading varieties with their long, flowing growth certainly are the best. They have been specially developed to give you that graceful, arching and swirling pattern complete with dazzling profusions of blooms.

Fortunately, plant breeders are clever in naming new varieties which they have developed. They usually name a new variety to indicate its color, growth habit, or other distinctive features. To find the cascading types, look at the names in seed catalogs or on seed packets in stores.

For red try Red Cascade. It has deep red, large-flowered blooms. Candy Apple is a vivid scarlet red, free-flowering, and more rain-resistant than other types if you get lots of showers where you live.

For pink or rose try Pink Cascade. It has extremely large blooms of carmine pink. Chiffon Cascade is light pastel pink with deeper pink veining and a creamy white throat.

Coral Cascade has extra-large coral

salmon blooms with a white throat. White Cascade, too, is large-flowered and bright white.

For blue and white, try Fandango with its deep blue and white blooms.

Some double-flowered petunias also can flow quite nicely in hanging baskets. As you try new types, you'll pick the ones that capture your vote for years to come.

STARTLING
SALVIAS

Among the flowers you can choose for the most brilliant reds and full, rich scarlets, salvias are usually the first to come to mind. These lovely plants deserve a place wherever you wish to create a dramatic effect in your garden.

Although they don't offer you the wide choice of colors you can find among many other types of flowers, such as petunias and zinnias, salvias are an asset for their dominant effect.

There are many native wild species of salvia in the western areas of the United States. In California there are about 15 named species. You can, if you like, choose to grow some of the wild ones that are

available from various wildflower farms and nurseries. In fact, there seems to be a wave of renewed interest in trying wildflower and naturalized gardens these days.

You can obtain the names of wildflower suppliers in most of the national and regional flower and garden magazines, usually available in your local library. *Horticulture* magazine, published by the Massachusetts Horticultural Society in Boston, always has a number of wildflower suppliers listed in its classified advertising section.

SALVIA HISTORY

Salvias are a large genus of plants. They belong to the Labiatae family, which contains more than 500 species found in the temperate and warmer parts of North and South America. This plant gets its name from the Latin word *salvo*, which relates to the healing properties of the garden sage, *Salvia officinalis*.

For centuries *Salvia officinalis* has been cultivated by good gardeners and good cooks. The reason is its flavor. The gray-green leaves have been used for many years as a tasty flavoring for meats.

A relative, *Salvia verbenaca*, is found wild in dry pastures in Great Britain. The thistle sage, *Salvia carduacea*, is cultivated in parts of the western United States for its white, wooly foliage and blue flowers. A Mexican relative, *Salvia columbariae*, and its close cousins are a source of chia—a strong flavoring used in a beverage in Mexico and the southwestern United States.

Traveling through California and other parts of the sunny West, you can find other salvias, from the black sage to the big flower sage. They are important as bee pollination plants.

These soft-wooded plants have never received the close attention from plant breeders that others have. However, the ornamental, cultivated red and scarlet varieties that have been developed are among the easiest annuals to grow. They are best as bedding plants or used in groups where you want a profusion of dramatic color.

GROW OTHER VARIETIES

Salvias are appreciated by many home gardeners for several reasons. They are one of the most brilliant of the bedding plants. They also begin bearing abundantly in early summer. They will continue to reward you with their delightful blooms all season until the first hard frost arrives.

You don't, however, have a wide choice of colors. No matter. You can blend salvias with other plants in different colors to achieve that sparkle and array of hues that you want.

Here are some of the best varieties for beds and borders, edgings and blendings, or as really spectacular potted plants to accent your outdoor living areas.

Blaze of Fire, the famous and striking Scarlet Sage, has excellent spike quality. Its early-flowering, brilliant scarlet blooms dominate a garden scene.

Early Bonfire is a mid-season variety. It

is free-flowering with long spikes of scarlet red.

Red Pillar, or Hot Jazz as it is also called, has solidly spiked blooms of rich scarlet with dark green foliage for beautiful and vivid contrast.

St. John's Fire is a compact early-flowering salvia in bright scarlet. It, too, has good spike quality, maturing about 10 inches.

For low-growing areas you can plant Scarlet Midget. This is among the best of the dwarf scarlet variety. It matures only 7 inches tall and is an early bloomer.

Blue salvias bear all summer and into late fall. In milder southern climates these can be treated as perennials. In northern areas the frost will usually kill them and require you to replant each year.

Try Farinacea Blue Bedder. It produces beautiful, deep Wedgwood-blue blooms. This variety is taller than others, maturing to 30 or so inches high. Patens will grow about 2 feet high. Its clear indigo-blue blooms are tubular and lipped.

To achieve the most vivid contrasts with these rich scarlet and blue salvias, consider matching or flanking them with the brightest white flowers. The true white asters will serve to set the brilliant reds of Scarlet Sage and its relatives off to striking and impressive advantage.

Double Multiflora and Giant Double petunias also blend well with salvias. Try Sonta, Snowberry Tart, and other all-white varieties. Glacier, Snow Lady, White Magic, or La Paloma among the Grandiflora petunias can provide that crisp, clear white to offset your salvias.

TRY HERBS

Once you enjoy Scarlet Sage, you'll probably become interested in growing other herbs as well. Herbs can put spice in your gardening life.

You'll need well-drained soil for most, and lots of sun. Herbs don't like wet feet, except mint, which prefers moist, shady areas.

Turn the soil as you would for a flower or vegetable garden. Work in some humus or compost. Most herbs have tiny seeds, so mix seed with sand for more even planting. Then cover with moist burlap until your herbs sprout. When they do, remove the burlap and water gently until they have established a firm roothold in their new home.

You can also purchase prestarted herb plants and set them into your desired location. Most people prefer to grow herbs near the kitchen door. That way, you can just

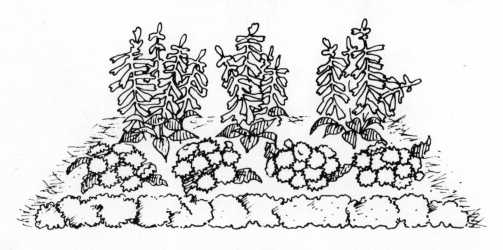

open the door and pick or snip a few leaves or sprigs to use in soups or salads or to flavor meats.

In addition to sage, you might try rosemary, tarragon, chives, basil, dill, parsley, and summer savory.

Most herbs are grown just for their value to flavor foods. Some, however, have attractive flowers.

In the fall, you can pick sprigs of herbs, tie them in a bunch, and hang them to dry in a cool, dry part of your home. When they have dried, crumble their leaves and store them in moisture-proof jars until you want to use them.

VEGETABLES

LUSCIOUS LETTUCE

Lettuce belongs in every garden. It is versatile and can be grown in rows, or special salad patches. You can grow it in pots and tubs and window boxes, too. The many forms of lettuce, from roundheads to curled and crinkly leafy types, make it a good addition to flower beds and borders. Although lettuce prefers cool weather to grow best, you can plan for early and late crops. Then, in the summer, you can switch to new varieties that withstand heat better without sending up seed stalks. You can also change to other types of lettuce, such as Bibb and Loosehead, to stretch your lettuce harvest all summer long. There are four basic types of lettuce: The familiar Crisphead type has outer green leaves and a nice white inside head. Butterhead develops well-folded heads, and looks like a small cabbage. Loosehead grows even in poor soil and warm weather. Cos, or Romaine, has upright growth with sweet, tender, green outer leaves hiding white inner leaves. Try several varieties. They're easy, tasty, and delicious. They're colorful and decorative as well.

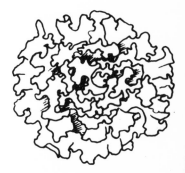

LETTUCE HISTORY

Lettuce, like many other popular vegetables, has its roots far back in ancient history. This age-old vegetable probably originated in western Asia. As its popularity grew, lettuce became well known throughout the ancient civilized world. It is recorded as a favorite of the Persians, Greeks, and Romans. Some old texts describe the decorative uses of lettuce. Bit by bit, or leaf by leaf, its health value and pleasing taste added to its reputation. Even before today's emphasis on vitamins and minerals, people knew that green leafy plants were nutritious. In fact, Romaine lettuce, also called Cos, was a real favorite among the ancient Romans. That's where it got its name. The family name of lettuce is Compositae. Its scientific name is *Lactuca satius*. This hardy annual grows best in cool weather, as we have mentioned. Warm weather causes it to send up slender stalks and go to seed. One type is grown mainly in China for the flavor of its stems. In Europe, gardeners prefer to grow the Butterhead type. In America, Crisphead lettuce is by far the most popular. Look up lettuce in your encyclopedia for more fun-packed knowledge about these popular plants. The more you know, the better you grow.

TRICKS WITH LETTUCE

Lettuce is the basic ingredient in most salads. Plan to have some ready every week. That does require well-timed planning. If you plant all the seeds at once, you get too much lettuce at one time, and none later. That can be disappointing, since you'll want lots of lettuce when tomatoes turn red and ripe. Try succession planting. Save some seed. Plant a dozen each week in peat pots or starter trays indoors. When these seedlings are the right size—one inch—to transplant, move them into your garden. Whenever you pick radishes, early lettuce, or anything, don't leave that spot unused. Replant it. Here's another idea. Build a salad pyramid. Fill with soil. Plant it with new lettuce started on your window so you can have it anytime.

MAKE TASTIER SALADS

Some folks like the cool, crackly taste of Crisphead lettuce. Others may favor the crunchy sweetness of Butterhead. Maybe you prefer the openness of Loosehead lettuce, or the distinct difference of Cos or Endive. There is a lot to like about the whole lettuce family.

CRISPHEAD

Crisphead is what you find in most stores. It has large, round, firm, and brittle heads. They snap when you cut into them. Great Lakes lettuce has a crackling habit. It forms large, tasty heads with white centers and dark green outer leaves in 90 days. Iceberg has smaller, more compact heads with crisp, tender silvery-white hearts. Imperial grows medium-size, compact heads with tender leaves in 85 days. Loosehead lettuce is easy and quick to grow, even in poor soil. It produces round, thick bunches of leaves even in warm weather. Green Ice has a dark green color and fringed leaves, and is ready in 45 days. Salad Bowl is crisp and tender with large green leaves. It can be picked in 45 days. There are many other tasty varieties you can find in seed stores and in mail-order catalogs. Experiment with any that appeal to you.

BUTTERHEAD

Butterhead lettuce forms well-folded heads, and looks like a small cabbage. It has light golden and yellow hearts with tender-tasting leaves. It doesn't like hot weather. Bibb has small heads that can be cut in half for individual servings. It stays crisp even when refrigerated. Buttercrunch has a large, heavier head. Leaves are thick, juicy, and crisp. Begin picking in 70 days. Tom Thumb is a small, compact lettuce that is ready in 65 days.

COS

Cos, or Romaine, lettuce has a sweet flavor. It grows upright with its head high, and is covered by medium green outer leaves. Good in northern areas. Paris White is a light green variety ready in 80 days.

ENDIVE

Endive is a lettuce relative, used for salads, but also may be cooked and served with butter sauce or cheese. Green Curles, also known as Giant Fringed Oyster, makes a tangy salad. All these varieties are good to look at and to eat. Get to know the entire lettuce family. They're fun to grow and treats to eat.

UNFRIENDLY INSECTS

Lettuce plants grow well for most gardeners. They should for you, too. But there are some insects and worms that like lettuce as much as you do. The cutworm is nasty. And it has a big appetite. Whenever there are unprotected new seedlings or transplants in a garden, it goes to work. A simple cardboard collar around transplants, extending 2 inches above and 2 inches below ground, frustrates the cutworms. Leafhoppers are occasional pests. The immature newly hatched nymphs suck plant juices. Several types of beetles also may decide to dine on your lettuce. You can usually see

their damage before they destroy the plant. Chewed holes in leaves are signs of beetle or worm damage. Little green or brown worms may also eat their fill of your lettuce. The same rules apply for lettuce as for any other vegetable. Keep looking for any insects or their damage. Pick off and dispose of any pests. Since worms may hide deep down inside lettuce leaves near the base of the plant, always wash lettuce and leafy vegetables thoroughly to rinse them away. In fact, you should always wash all vegetables clean to get rid of dust and soil that cling to damp vegetables.

ENJOY WINDOW SILL SALADS

Everyone loves green plants. Today people are growing all types of house plants on window sills, porches, and all around their homes. Why not grow lettuce as attractive house plants? Several types do well indoors. All you need are some pots or bowls, gravel for a layer in the bottom, and soil. Any potted plant needs drainage so excess water won't damage the roots. Use containers about 6 inches deep. Plant seeds, and remove all except the strongest 1 or 2 seedlings. You can use transplants from starter trays. Fertilizer is seldom needed, since only 1 or 2 plants will mature in 50 days or so.

Loosehead lettuce varieties are best. They grow faster. Enjoy different textures, shapes, and colors at your windows by selecting several Loosehead varieties. Green Ice has dark, glossy green leaves with wavy, fringed margins. Salad Bowl lettuce has deeply lobed leaves. They are medium green. They sparkle as plants, and give a colorful extra touch to your salads. Lettuce can add beauty and color, as well as taste, to your indoor gardening. More people every day are learning that a garden is anywhere you can grow some plants to please you. Use your imagination, and good growing.

LANDSCAPE WITH LETTUCE

There is no rule that says you can't grow vegetables and flowers together. For some reason people seem to think flowers should be in one bed and vegetables somewhere else. The fact is, adding flowers to the vegetable garden really brightens that area. Some flowers also chase away those harmful, unwanted insects. Interplanting vegetables like lettuce with flowers adds leafy textures, shades, and forms to accent the flowers more. Select colorful, curled, frilled, or lobed-leaf types. Then plant low-growing pansies, marigolds, alyssum, dwarf asters, or whatever flowers you wish to mix and match with a tasty salad patch.

DOORSTEP SALAD PATCH

Here's how to grow one. The closer to the kitchen, the better. Just a few square feet will do. Dig the soil a foot deep. Improve it if necessary. Plant a tomato or two. As they grow, tie them to tall poles so they grow up. Around the tomatoes, add lettuce plants. Try some radishes, too. Mulch them all, and water once a week. A cup or two of plant food monthly keeps them growing. A kitchen-door salad patch seems to get better care. You pass it every day, so you can keep a better eye on it to give your mini-garden close attention. You'll also spot vegetables just as they ripen. This will make for tastier eating.

LIVELY, LUSCIOUS LETTUCE

Crisp and snappy lettuce can add sparkle to any meal. Here's how you can use all types of lettuce in salads, sandwiches, and special ways to make meals more festive.

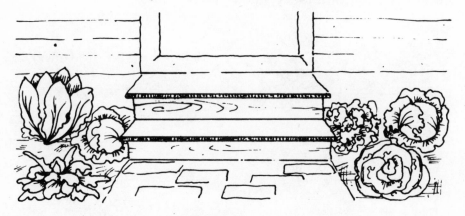

SANDWICHES

For school lunches or on weekends, too, put a few lettuce leaves on sandwich meats. They add a crisp, moist texture and vitamins, too. Surprise your parents with your own BLT. Slice red, ripe, juicy tomatoes and add some loose-leaf or Bibb lettuce leaves between warm brown toast. Add bacon slices. That's a treat for anyone.

LETTUCE REFRESHER

Wash a head of lettuce and put it in the crisper compartment of your refrigerator. When it's cool, peel off several leaves. Arrange them into a bed on a plate. Add a peach or pear half in the center. Then place a spoonful of cottage cheese in the center of the fruit.

TOSSED SALADS

Just about everyone loves salads. Let your imagination wander free. Select several types of lettuce. Wash the heads and leaves well. Then cut or break the leaves, and put them into a big salad bowl. Peel an apple, core it, and cut it into small chunks. Chop up a celery stalk or two. Add juicy slices of tomato, or tiny, bite-size, whole tomatoes. Include a few bits of onion, or other fresh garden greens. Add several carrot sticks. Experiment all you want.

LETTUCE AND EGGS

Hard boil some eggs and let them cool. Wash a head of lettuce. Cool it. Then make a bed of lettuce from tender leaves. Quarter or slice the eggs. Place them on the lettuce. Add olive halves for tasty decoration.

HEARTS OF LETTUCE

Pick the best, most tender heads of lettuce in your garden. Wash them well. Remove the outer leaves. Then cut the heads into quarters. Place on salad plates and top with salad dressing of your choice. There are hundreds of ways to make salads with combinations of greens, vegetables, and dressings.

GROW
DELICIOUS
TOMATOES

There's nothing like rich, red, ripe tomatoes, picked plump right off the vine. They taste so good that they are the most popular vegetable in America, year after year. You can grow delicious, vine-ripe tomatoes in your own garden, or even in a patio planter or pot indoors. Tomatoes are so versatile that they are used in cooking all over the world. By following the tasty recipes at the end of this chapter, you, too, can make juice, sauce, stuffed tomatoes, and other dishes from your tomatoes.

Growing tomatoes is easier than you think. Once you pick the right location, plant and fertilize, control insects and weeds, you can grow the tastiest, largest, and best tomatoes in town.

TOMATO HISTORY

Tomatoes are native to South America. Indians of the Andes Mountains grew them in prehistoric times. As tribes migrated they took tomatoes along and introduced them to Mexico some 2,000 years ago. From there, Spanish explorers introduced tomatoes into Europe during the 16th century. Soon after, tomatoes were being widely grown in Italy. In fact, Italian tomatoes are still famous today. Although tomatoes were enjoyed in Europe for years, it was not until the 19th century that people in the United States would eat them. For some unexplained reason, people here thought they were poisonous. Maybe that's because tomatoes are a member of the nightshade family of plants, which does include poisonous types.

Today we all realize tomatoes are healthful and delicious. They are rich in vitamins A and C. They're so tasty and good that tomatoes are grown in almost all the cooler areas around the world today. In scientific terms, tomatoes are members of the Solanaceae family. Although tomatoes are classified as a fruit, an 1893 definition says tomatoes are fruits when they are eaten out of hand or fresh, but are vegetables when they are cooked.

NEW VARIETIES/BIG YIELDS

You can grow giant 3-pound tomatoes or tiny bite-size ones. Most are red, but there are pink and yellow round types, too. If you like, try red or yellow plum-, pear-, or cherry-shaped tomatoes. On these pages you'll find some of the best and easiest to grow, including some really terrific new hybrids. Hybrid tomatoes have important advantages. A hybrid is the result of crossing two different varieties. The new hybrid

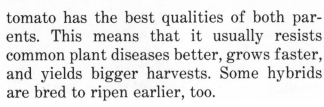

tomato has the best qualities of both parents. This means that it usually resists common plant diseases better, grows faster, and yields bigger harvests. Some hybrids are bred to ripen earlier, too.

GIANT-SIZE

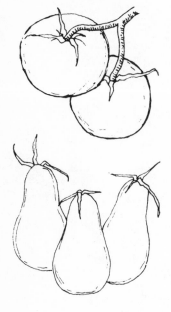

Big Boy Giant Hybrid will produce lots of the largest tomatoes. It is smooth, firm, and scarlet red, with thick walls and meaty flesh of fine flavor. It ripens in 80 days. Better Boy Hybrid bears bright red, delicious tomatoes up to 1 pound each, all season long. It resists diseases and matures in 75 days. Beefsteak has large, deep-scarlet fruit. This standard type yields vigorous vines of huge scarlet tomatoes in 80 days. Early Girl Hybrid produces lots of regular-size bright red tomatoes 50 days after planting. Spring Giant Hybrid gives heavy yields of bright rich fruit about 8 ounces big. It won All-America honor for its ability to grow well easily, and provides tomatoes in 65 days. These heavy yields are great if you have limited growing space.

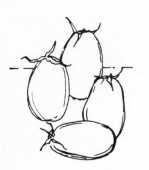

BITE-SIZE

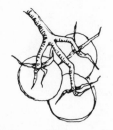

Pixie Hybrid grows and ripens quickly. You get lots of cherry-size tomatoes within 52 days of planting. You can grow it outdoors in the garden, or year-round indoors. Tiny Tim is a scarlet, fine-textured hybrid with the ability to bear many tomatoes in 55 days on plants only 15 inches tall. Basket Pak is perfect for salads, with rich, red, juicy flavor all season. It's ready in 75 days.

OTHER COLORS AND SIZES

Jubilees are golden-orange tomatoes that yield well and ripen in 72 days. Ponderosa is purplish pink with large flavorful tomatoes weighing a pound or more. Yellow Pear and Yellow Plum tomatoes are tasty. They look like the fruits for which they are named. Roma and San Marzano are Italian-type tomatoes with small, firm, red fruits that make great tomato sauce. There are many other varieties you can try. All are interesting and different.

UNFRIENDLY INSECTS

Some insects and worms prefer to eat your ripe tomatoes. Good for them, but bad for you.

It pays to know your insect and worm enemies so that you can identify them and take action early before they start chewing into your valued plants.

The tomato fruitworm is round and fat, about 1½ inches long. It chews the actual tomato. The tomato hornworm has spots, and is even chubbier and greener. It has a horn at one end that marks it well. The cutworm is another villain. It chews through tender seedling stalks. A simple cardboard collar around transplants can keep it out.

Aphids are sucking pests. They drain sap, making the leaves curl, reducing plant strength, and encouraging disease.

Other insects may attack your tomatoes from time to time. It pays to check your plants each week. If insects or worms are in sight, it's time to attack.

Hand-pick enemy worms off the plants. Small white aphids usually lurk beneath the leaves. If you can't control pests by hand use pesticides.

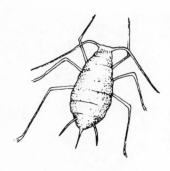

TRY INDOOR TOMATOES

Today you can enjoy tomatoes year round. Tasty new varieties need little space to grow indoors. They grow well in pots, tubs, or even in hanging baskets. All you need is sun, soil, water, and some tender loving care.

Select a container that allows for good drainage. An 8-inch pot is fine—measure the diameter from side to side at the open top. Put an inch of gravel in the bottom. Next comes the soil. You can buy it premixed or make your own. Take one part vermiculite, then add one part peat moss. If you have compost, add one part to the mixture. Mix well with a spoonful of 5-10-5 fertilizer per gallon of soil mix.

Start seeds right in this mix. As they sprout, remove the smallest, leaving the best to mature and bear. Water every week. Add a spoonful of liquid plant food each month. Keep your tomatoes in a sunny window. Southern exposure is best; eastern exposure, next best.

Tiny Tim, Pixie, and other varieties have been developed for indoor growing. In less than two months you'll see small fruits appear. Soon after that you'll be picking red, ripe tomatoes even on the coldest days of winter. That's a treat for everyone.

TRICKS WITH TOMATOES

Tomatoes will climb fences, thrive in wire hoops, grow vine-ripe even in the fall if protected from frost. Try these tricks yourself for fun.

When transplanting, lay tall or spindly seedlings on the ground. Bend the top portion up gently. Cover the root ball and lower stem with soil. Roots form all along the stem to get plants growing faster. Then cut old wire coat hangers. Make hoops and cover them with clear plastic film held in place by soil. This will guard plants against chilly spring nights. Each sunny morning open the tent so air can circulate. Each cool evening re-cover the plants until warmer weather. Then remove hoops and plastic completely.

Make a cylinder of old fencing wire. Make a hoop 2 to 3 feet in diameter. Place this over a tomato plant. As it grows tall, branches grow out to support the plant upright. You'll be able to find tomatoes more easily. Tomatoes are cleaner than if plants ramble along the ground naturally.

In the fall, position two old storm windows like an A-frame with plastic sides over several plants. This keeps fall frost off plants. Tomatoes bear in cool weather if leaves aren't nipped by frost. It's tricky, but try to forestall frost-kill.

TASTY TOMATO TREATS

Once you have grown rich, red, ripe tomatoes and enjoyed them fresh from your vines, it's time to try some tomato recipes as well. Here are several you should like:

HOMEMADE TOMATO JUICE

Use as many ripe tomatoes as you wish—check the size of the pot you intend to use. First dip tomatoes in hot water. This loosens the skins. Then peel them. Next, cut them into quarters. Put them in a pot without water—just use the natural juice. Bring to a boil. Simmer for 5 minutes, then strain. Finally, pour the juice into clean freezer jars or containers. Leave an inch at the top. Seal and freeze.

STEWED TOMATOES

Peel tomatoes, after dipping in hot water to loosen skin, and cut into quarters. For every 6 large tomatoes, add 1 stalk of celery, 1 clove, and 1 teaspoon minced onion. Put in a pot and heat slowly. Stir to keep from scorching. Add ¾ teaspoon salt, 2 teaspoons brown sugar, ¼ teaspoon chopped parsley, and 1 tablespoon butter. Cook for about 10 minutes. You can freeze this, too. Think of delicious stewed tomatoes on a cold winder day. What a treat!

TUNA-STUFFED TOMATOES

Pick your best and biggest tomatoes and wash thoroughly. Then cut out the core so you can put in the stuffing. Mix 1 can of white tuna meat with 1 heaping tablespoon of mayonnaise. Stir in 1 stalk of chopped celery. Add ¼ cup chopped onion. Fill the open centers of the tomatoes with the tuna mix. Place the stuffed tomatoes on a bed of crisp green lettuce and chill. You can also use other fish. Salmon, shrimp, or tuna makes a flavorful lunch that's cool and refreshing.

SIMPLE SLICED TOMATOES

Pick big beauties and wash thoroughly. Chill in refrigerator. When ready to serve, slice crosswise and arrange attractively on plate.

You'll find dozens of other lively recipes in cookbooks. Once you grow tasty tomatoes, test your talent in finding new ways to eat them. Look up recipes so you can put some tomatoes in the freezer or on the canning shelf to enjoy all year long. They are welcome as an addition to any meal, or as a nutritious snack. You'll be pleasantly surprised to see your tomatoes on the table. They will remind you of your garden.

PICK
A PECK OF
PICKLES

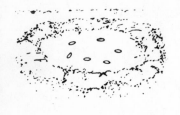

Before you can enjoy tasty, crispy, perky pickles, you must grow the cucumbers. That's where pickles come from. Cukes are easy to raise, and fun to eat in many ways. In fact, cucumbers have been popular for centuries. You can grow them in rows, plant them in hills, or even train them to climb a fence or mount a trellis. Although they are a vine, cucumbers take up little space. One big advantage is their ability to yield—week after week, all season long. They will surprise you. One morning you will find just a few tiny cukes. By evening, those small cucumbers may have grown several inches longer. Cucumbers are fun to grow because quick growth gives fast results.

Of course, you can perfect your pickle-making talents later on. Cucumbers respond fondly to your tender loving care. They like lots to drink and thrive best when you provide enriched soil with compost and organic matter in it. You, too, can pick your own peck of pickles this year.

CUCUMBER HISTORY

Cucumbers trace their history to the glorious days of ancient Rome and far beyond. Tales are told of one famed Roman emperor who just couldn't satisfy his hunger for pickles.

Throughout the years, especially in the Middle Ages, cucumbers were popular. One of the main reasons was that they could be preserved. That provided people with another method of storing food for winter eating. Even the great emperor Charlemagne insisted on growing cucumbers in his garden back in the 9th century.

Cucumbers were introduced to the New World by early explorers. Some tales tell that Christopher Columbus also enjoyed pickled pleasures. So fond of them was he that legend says he ordered cucumber seeds brought on his voyages. That's how, history reports, cucumbers first arrived in America. Since then, cucumbers have been greatly improved. New varieties are more flavorful, grow faster, bear earlier, and provide us all with a wide choice of hardy, fruitful cukes. We can enjoy them in so many tasty ways. Now, you too can have your own taste of history from a cucumber patch.

TRICKS WITH CUCUMBERS

You can have fun experimenting with your cucumber patch. Try these easy tricks. One morning, mark the middle of several small cucumbers with chalk or a magic marker. Measure their total length. The following day, check their growth and measure them again. You'll be surprised how quickly these vegetables grow.

You may also wish to try comparison tests. Soak one hill well. Put less water on the next hill. Compare the size, growth rate, and total crop you get from each.

To grow giant cukes for fun, bury a jar in the ground. Slit one vine and insert a fiberglass wick into it. Fasten it securely with electrical tape. Put the other end of the wick in a jar of water. Keep it full and compare the cukes on that vine with those nearby.

TRY DIFFERENT VARIETIES

Cucumbers are crisp and nice for salads and relishes. You have a wide choice. There are two types of cukes—either with white or black spines. Both taste fine.

HYBRIDS

New hybrids offer sweeter flavor, fewer seeds, and resistance to some cucumber diseases. That's helpful. M & M Hybrid grows fast and furiously. It yields slender cukes in 60 days. Burpless Hybrid is tasty, easy to digest, and matures in 60 days, too. Victory variety vines yield heavily—with dark green fruit for slices, or as fresh sticks for party dips.

STANDARD CUKES

Sunnybrook can be used for pickling when picked young and tender, or for salads. It can grow a foot long, but is best when half that size, which it reaches by 60 days. Straight Eight has deep-green color and grows well. It ripens in 55 days.

PICKLING CUKES

Pickling varieties are vigorous and yield heavily all season. You can gather fruit at all stages. If you want smaller pickles, then simply pick the cukes when they are tiny. Any type of cucumber can be eaten fresh as long as you pick fruits when they are young and tender. Don't worry about depleting your supply. With cucumbers, the more you pick, the more you'll grow.

Some varieties are designed to grow rapidly for larger, dill-type pickles. Pioneer matures in 50 days to give you crisp, dark-green, cylindrical-shaped cukes. It's fine for all types of pickling or relish-making fun. East Indian Gherkin is the special one to grow if you prefer those tiny, tasty gherkin pickles. It will produce bushels for your pickling pleasure week after week after week.

Unless you have a special purpose in mind, a standard or hybrid cucumber variety will probably perform quite well in your home garden. Remember that cucumbers of all types need lots of water, especially at fruiting time. Watering twice a week is good.

When they are well fed and watered, cucumbers will continue to set blooms, fruit, and bear. For this reason, you may not wish to plant all the seeds in a typical seed packet. Two hills of cucumbers with several plants in each hill will produce all you'll need. You can plant more, but be prepared to pick lots more cucumbers.

UNFRIENDLY INSECTS

Years ago, cucumbers were harder to grow. Today, better and hardier varieties have been developed by plant breeders. These varieties do resist common diseases. They have built-in resistance to mildew, wilt, and mosaic disease. In addition, fungicides can help prevent these problems just in case they occur. Always ask your parents or another adult to help you before using any type of spray or dust.

Several insects may bother your cucumbers. The main enemy is the striped cucumber beetle. Almost overnight these pests may destroy new seedlings just as they push through the soil. They cut stems and eat the leaves. These beetles also may pass along plant diseases. Underground they damage plant roots, causing plants to wilt and die.

In southern states, the pickleworm may be more common. It hatches on leaves, then bores into cucumbers and squash. Keep close watch over your cukes. Any time you see pests, pick them off. If you don't, they'll destroy your vegetables. Battle bugs regularly. Make sure you spray under vines, where many of these harmful pests stay hidden. That way you get rid of them completely.

CLIMBING/HANGING CUKES

Cucumbers will climb if given good support. New bush varieties can be grown in hanging baskets. The Cherokee cucumber is one variety that will grow in pots. It produces 7-inch-long cukes on its 3-foot bushy vines. It's great for a hanging basket. Put gravel in the bottom—about an inch. Add soil, and plant the seeds. It helps to hang strong cord from the pot so vines can grasp it with their wraparound tendrils as they overflow from the hanging planter.

Erect a pole in the center of a large redwood planter. Tie strings from its top to the sides of the planter. Add a gravel layer and soil, and plant your seeds. As cukes sprout, they'll reach for the sky, climbing up the strings to form a teepee of foliage. It's really decorative, too.

When you grow vegetables in containers, remember, that you must provide more plant food and water more regularly than you would if they were growing in the ground. Their roots can't go in search of their food and drink as garden plants can. Use a good liquid plant fertilizer, mixed according to label directions, to keep your container cucumbers thriving. You can also use timed-release granular fertilizer.

Some gardeners don't grow cucumbers

because they think the vines require too much room. True, they'll roam all around the garden if you let them. Here's how to teach them to behave:

Erect a wire fence to let cucumbers climb. They will do so quite easily. Place poles every 4 to 6 feet. Attach the fencing securely. By the time fall arrives, just roll the fencing around the poles and store it for next season.

Another way is to build cucumbers their own growing box. Add an inch of gravel first, then soil and seeds. If the vines grow too far afield, prune the ends or redirect them where you want them to grow. Pruning does reduce your crop of cukes, but at times a compromise is necessary.

A third way to give your plants the room they need is to let them climb onto tall plants such as corn. You can also interplant them between tall crops so the vines shade the earth almost like a mulch to smother weeds. Cukes will climb corn and roam around the stalks, too. Whenever you can get cukes climbing and off the ground, you'll reduce the chance of their rotting on wet ground. Keep this in mind for all climbing soft-fruited plants, and you'll get more total harvest.

WAYS TO ENJOY YOUR CUKES

Just about everyone enjoys pickles. Once you have grown cucumbers, you too can turn them into delicious pickles. Perhaps some simple ways to enjoy cucumbers should come first.

CUCUMBER STICKS

Pick several cukes from your garden. Remove the skin with a paring knife. Cut in lengths. Sprinkle with salt and pepper to taste. Serve chilled.

FILLED CUCUMBERS

Pare several cucumbers. Cut them in halves lengthwise. Remove seeds and fill with tuna fish, chopped chicken, or any filling that pleases you. Chill and serve on a leaf of crisp lettuce.

QUICK PICKLE SLICES

Pare 4 medium cucumbers. Cut off the ends. Slice very thin and put in a bowl. Mix 2 cups cider vinegar with 2 cups water. Add 2 tablespoons sugar. Stir well to dissolve the sugar. Add this to the cucumber slices. Cover and allow to chill overnight. This recipe is quick, easy, and delicious. Try it as a surprise for your parents, and watch how pleased they'll be. You'll be proud of your new cooking skills.

BREAD AND BUTTER PICKLES

This recipe is more difficult, so ask Mom or Dad or an older friend to help. It's easy but takes time. Wash 1 gallon of medium cucumbers. Peel 6 large or 12 small onions.

Cut cukes and onions into really thin slices. Put in a bowl. Add ½ cup coarse salt, cover, and put in the refrigerator for about 3 hours. Then wash in cold water. Wash and drain again. Next, pour 5 cups cider vinegar into a pot. Add 5 cups of brown sugar. Add 1½ teaspoons allspice, 2 tablespoons mustard seed, and a 1-inch piece of stick cinnamon. Bring this mixture to a boil. Add the cucumber and onion slices. Slowly heat to a boil, but do not boil. Remove from the heat and pour into clean jars. Cool. Ask your parents to help you seal the jars for longer preservation and more pickle-eating pleasure. Put into the refrigerator. In about a week you can enjoy your bread and butter pickles.

There are many different ways to make relishes and types of pickles. If you have followed the growing methods suggested in this chapter, you will have many extra cucumbers to pickle. Ask your parents to help you plan a pickling party. Then all of you can enjoy cucumbers for many months to come.

A
BOUNTY OF
BEANS

Tasty green beans are one of the most popular and easiest to grow of all vegetables. Because seeds are so large and have enough food stored in them to get plants started well, all you need do is provide the right sunny location, well-drained soil, and a helping hand with fertilizer along the bush bean row or around pole bean hills in your garden.

There are many types of beans and a wide choice of varieties of each type. Beans grow quickly and bear abundantly. For these reasons you should plan to grow successions of beans. This means don't plant all the seeds from one packet at one time unless you plan to can or freeze them. Instead, plant a row or several short rows. Then, several weeks later, when first rows are growing well, plant more. This way you can pick young, tender beans week after week. When first rows have finished bearing, simply pull out the plants and reuse that part of your garden. You can plant other crops, such as lettuce, carrots, cabbage, or more beans as you wish.

The important point is to keep every part

of your garden growing so you can have good eating from early in the season right into fall until frost nips your tender plants and cancels the growing year. For lots of growing fun and tasty eating, too, try beans this year.

BEAN HISTORY

Since prehistoric times, beans have provided food for man. They are rich in carbohydrates, proteins, plus minerals and Vitamin B. Broad beans were eaten in Europe since mankind first began growing crops. Beans also were cultivated by earliest civilization in Mexico and Peru.

Beans are pod-bearing plants called legumes. In addition to producing their prized beans, these plants also help enrich soil. Roots of bean plants play host to nitrogen-fixing bacteria. As plants grow, these valuable bacteria take nitrogen from the air and convert it to soluble nitrogen compounds, and capture and "fix" nitrogen

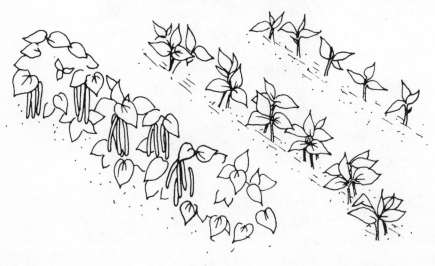

on root nodules. When the plants die, you can turn or till them underneath the soil so the "fixed" nitrogen will enrich it.

Over the centuries many types of beans have been developed. You can eat them fresh or cooked in various ways, or you can store them by freezing, canning, or picking and drying. Since beans have long been valued for food, they are grown in all parts of the world.

Beans belong to the Leguminosae family, and a big family it is indeed. From simple green snap beans popular with most families, you can explore a whole world of beans, in all sizes, colors, and tastes. Snap beans were once called string beans. But plant breeders realized that people didn't like the stringy fibers on these beans. Today they have improved beans so that the fibers are more tender and the beans, when picked young and tender, snap easily in half or in pieces.

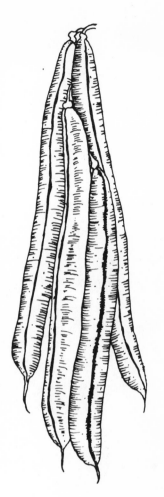

INSECT ENEMIES

Probably the best-known insect pest of beans is the notorious Mexican bean beetle. One day you see your healthy, happy beans growing well. The next day, or so it seems, there will be holes in several of the leaves. Within a week or so, if not controlled, these hungry, bean beetles can chew away many of the bean plant leaves. They'll even sink their teeth into the beans.

Fortunately, these pests are easy to spot. Look under leaves every few days. If you see tiny clusters of whitish eggs or tiny,

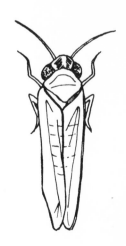

furry larvae, you have been invaded. The adult beetles that flew into your garden to lay their eggs may be crawling over the foliage, too.

Larvae hatch in 5 to 14 days. They feed beneath leaves and pass through four stages, each larger than the previous one. Full-grown larvae enter the pupa, or inactive, stage after 30 days and emerge adult beetles 10 days later. Adults begin to lay eggs and that starts the cycle again.

You can hand-pick larvae off leaves and scrape away eggs. Your best bet is a simple pesticide dust or spray, following the rules for proper use of insecticides.

If you plant beans early, you can often harvest one crop before beetles strike. Then remove the bean plants. In midsummer you can plant beans again and with luck get them harvested before any beetles return to nibble your crop.

BEANS FOR SPECIAL STUDY

You can have fun studying beans and can even try some experiments at home or in your classroom. Beans have large seeds compared to many other types of plants. That makes them easier to handle, grow, and study.

Select several clear-plastic drinking cups and fill them with a mixture of equal parts sand, soil, and peat moss. In each cup, plant one bean seed of any type you want. Try different types to compare their growing habits.

You may find it easier to use two pieces

of blotting paper. Place bean seeds on one sheet, then cover with another sheet. Keep the blotting paper moist so seeds sprout and begin to develop between the sheets. They will dry out in warm rooms, so be sure to add water daily.

Whether you grow your bean seeds in blotting paper, cups, or pots, you'll discover several things as you watch nature's mysteries unfold.

After the bean seed has absorbed water, its skin will wrinkle. Within a day or so an embryo root called a radicle will emerge. Even if you planted the seed upside down, this tiny root will grow downward. It knows which way is up and which way is down. Within a few more days, you'll see tiny secondary roots form. In soil, these anchor the plant and begin to seek moisture and plant food. A few days later, a portion of the root will arch upward to become the stem. As it grows and straightens, this stem will pull the bean seed free of the soil. Then, before your eyes the seed will split and open. As it does, you'll see tiny leaves emerge. Soon they'll enlarge and grow. In time, after the seed has supplied the baby plant with its supply of stored food, it will shrivel and drop off.

You can continue by studying different types of beans or arrange various kinds of fertilizers to learn more about how plants grow. Try experiments with beans for show and tell or science fair projects as well. They're quite revealing.

FUN WITH BEANS

Some beans grow on bushes. Others grow sky high as pole beans. If you have limited space, you can grow lots of beans on poles, fences, or on a trellis.

You might enjoy growing a pole bean teepee. One way to make a teepee frame is by using at least three poles, about 6 to 8 feet tall. Tie the tops together with string. Then, plant your bean seeds in a circle around each pole. As they grow, you'll see the growing tips reach out to wrap themselves around each pole. Within weeks they will have climbed to the top. You'll have full vines overhead and shady room to hide inside while you just reach out and pick snap beans to eat—if you have not used pesticides.

You can also grow beans on wire or weave a string fence to let your beans do their climbing. You must provide some support for pole beans. Otherwise, they'll just ramble around the ground and not produce a good quantity of tender, sweet, clean, fresh beans.

Push several 6- to 8-foot poles into the ground 3 feet apart. Several vines of the better varieties will produce beans aplenty. You can stretch a wire fence between several boards driven into the ground. Or, you can make a string trellis. Just tie stout cord between two sturdy poles 6 to 10 feet apart, at the bottom and top of the poles. Then, tie cords a foot apart along the top and attach to the bottom cord. You can also tie some string diagonally. Your pole beans will take hold and easily climb your inexpensive string fence. At season's end, just cut the cords, remove the string, and put your vines into the compost pile to rot into the soil, improving humus for your garden next year.

MORE FUN WITH BEANS

Once you have enjoyed growing green beans, try your skill at growing some other types. You will be pleased at how well different types will grow for you. You can grow beans that produce seeds of different colors, from white and green and spotted to yellow, tan, pink, red, brown, purple, and even black. For the best food value and high protein, you can try broad beans, lima beans, tiny Oriental mung beans, or the best protein beans, soybeans. Broad and lima beans contain up to 25 percent protein. Soybeans are widely grown by farmers around the entire world for their even higher—up to 35 percent—protein content. In recent years, many people have realized that soybeans are a very valuable natural

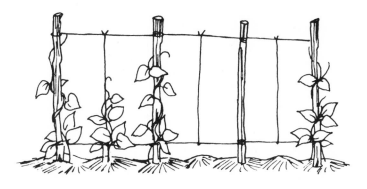

health food because they have so much protein. They will grow well in most gardens.

However, instead of eating them and the pods as you do with snap beans, you must let them dry right on the vines. Then shell and cook the beans. They have a nice nutty taste.

Try tiny seeded mung beans, too. Many people prefer to eat them as young, tender bean sprouts. They usually are the bean sprouts used in popular Oriental dishes.

To surprise friends, try growing yard-long beans. These pole beans will mature at least 1 foot long. With adequate water and fertilizer, they can grow as long as 3 feet. For best eating, pick when smaller. To be a champion bean grower, let them grow as long as they will.

BEAN VARIETIES

BUSH-TYPE GREEN SNAP BEANS

Tenderpod has wonderful flavor and is a highly popular bean for its tenderness and lack of fibers or strings. An All-America winner, it yields heavily from 50 days. Beans are 4 to 6 inches long, smooth and slightly curved at the ends.

Bountiful is best for French-style cutting. It is a popular, all-purpose, flat green bean 6 to 7 inches long, stringless and broad.

Royalty is a purple pod bush bean, delicious fresh or frozen. It grows well in colder areas and is somewhat resistant to bean beetles. Pods are round, purple, tender, and stringless. It matures in 50 days and turns dark green when cooked.

Romano bush beans have the fine flavor of pole Romanos, but in bush growth habit. They mature two weeks before pole beans— in about 50 days—and produce broad, flat, medium green pods 4 to 5 inches long.

Tendercrop is tasty, with dark green, tender, smooth and round pods. It matures in 55 days and has the advantage of resisting common bean diseases.

YELLOW BUSH BEANS

Brittle Wax matures in 55 days, yields well, has fine snapability and good taste. The lemon-yellow pods, 6 to 7 inches long, are good fresh, frozen, or canned.

Goldcrop Wax is an All-America winner with erect growth, heavy yield, and resistance to common bean diseases. It freezes and cans well.

POLE BEANS

Kentucky Wonder has been an old standby in many gardens. It matures in 65 days and has distinctive flavor, both in its fresh pods and its dried, light brown seeds used as shell beans later in the season. It bears heavily with clusters of 6- to 9-inch-long meaty, tender, brittle beans. It's best picked 4 to 7 inches long. A rust-resistant variety is available.

Golden pole beans mature in 60 or so days, with meaty, tasty, wide, flat, yellow pods. You'll find this type seems to form a bushy growth, and then grows tall.

Romano is an Italian pole bean that

matures in 70 days. It's distinctive flavor and heavy yields have made it popular for home gardens. Vines carry many long, wide-podded beans that are especially tender and meaty. It also is good for freezing.

Consult seed catalogs for the many other types of bush green and wax snap beans as well as the improved types of pole beans.

BUSH SHELL BEANS

You can try several types of beans for shelling and drying. Red Kidney, White Marrowfat, and Long Pod English broad beans offer new taste sensations from your home garden. Dwarf Horticultural is a green shell type, delicious dried and cooked.

DISPLAY YOUR BEAN SKILLS

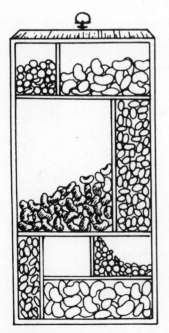

Here's an idea to decorate your room with beans. First, you must grow several different types. Select from seed catalogs to obtain those that have different colored seeds when mature. Grow whichever you like and enjoy eating them. But, leave about a dozen or so of each type to mature, partially dry, on the bush or vine.

When they have dried, shell them and dry fully on a cookie tin in the sun for a day. Then, design a simple bean or seed display box. Cut several pieces of wood. Sand edges smooth. Then assemble pieces as illustrated here to form compartments of different sizes and shapes. Next, fill these compartments with your different colored and shaped seeds. Finally, cover the box with a sturdy plexiglass sheet or pane of glass and attach a frame around it. This makes a conversation-piece display for hanging on your wall or placing on your desk or bureau.

SNAPPY BEAN TRICKS

You don't need much room to have fun with beans. They grow quickly if you remember to wait until after the last spring frost to plant them. Beans are tender and will be killed by frost. Plant after the soil is thoroughly warm, in hills, in rows, and even in a window sill garden. Beans provide bright green foliage, so you might even try them as a bed or border interplanted with flowers. They'll provide a lush background for petunias, pansies, marigolds, and zinnias. Because beans grow so quickly, you can be picking your first beans within 45 days from the time you plant the seeds. They'll bear for several weeks. Then, you can simply remove the plants. That leaves room for your colorful flowers to fill out and take advantage of the extra mid-season growing room to bloom better.

Try a tub of beans. Put an inch-deep layer of gravel in the bottom of a tub, wooden barrel, or other sturdy container. Then, add good garden soil to within a half-inch of the top.

Place a pole in the center. Next, tie strings or brightly colored decorative cord from top of the pole to points around the rim of your container. Plant pole bean seeds. As they climb, you'll have a tall and lovely flowering vine that will reward you all season long with tender, tasty beans right in your porch, balcony, or patio planter garden.

BEAN RECIPES

You can enjoy your garden beans in many ways. Cookbooks tell you how to prepare them as well as pickle them. Here are some easy recipes for you to try this season.

FRESH BEAN SALAD

Pick tender young beans that snap easily. Pick them before seeds begin to swell inside the pod. For most varieties this is 4 to 5 inches long. Then, wash well to remove any garden soil or pesticide residues that may have been sprayed on your beans to control pests.

Pick some lettuce, a tomato or two, some young carrots and radishes. Wash all well. Then, slice carrots and radishes, and cut beans into inch-long pieces. Chop lettuce, cut tomatoes into bite-size pieces, and mix all ingredients in a salad bowl. Then, add your favorite salad dressing for a refreshing, nutritious treat.

COOKED SNAP BEANS

The easiest way to cook green or yellow snap beans is to boil them. But don't make the same mistake so many people do. Even adults who have been cooking for years tend to boil beans and other vegetables in too much water and for too long. By overcooking you lose much of the valuable vitamins and minerals from your vegetables.

Just pick enough beans for one meal. Pour enough water into the pot to cover the bottom about an inch deep. Put your washed, cut beans into boiling water and cover. Cook for no more than 10 minutes, or until your beans are tender. Younger beans cook faster. This low-water cooking preserves both flavor and food value.

EASY FREEZING

Since you will find that beans bear abundantly, you'll most likely have lots of extra beans from your home garden. Freezing is a simple way to store beans for eating fun all year until the next garden season.

Pick and wash the tender beans well. Cut or slice them first if you wish. Then, place them in a metal colander. Boil water and place the colander of beans into it. Blanch for 5 minutes. Then, remove and cool in cold water for 5 minutes. Blanching is not really cooking. It is a process needed to stop the action of enzymes in the beans (or other vegetables) before freezing. After beans have cooled, remove them and pack in plastic freezer bags or containers and place on the freezing tray of your family's home freezer. When you want to enjoy them some winter day, just remove, drop into boiling water, and cook till tender.

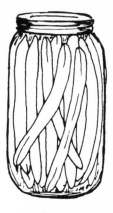

CORN—
THE CASH
CROP

Corn is America's largest and oldest crop. There are many types, from the delicious sweet corn grown in home gardens to the field corn used for livestock. More than 4 billion bushels of corn are grown in the United States each year. Although the coarser field corn is manufactured into many foods, most people are familiar with the sweet corn that does so well in home gardens.

Corn is easy to grow, although it does take a bit more room than many people have to spare. However, over the years plant breeders have developed not only sweeter corn, but early maturing types and dwarf varieties that bear several ears on one stalk. With these developments, you can enjoy the sweetest treat from your own garden.

There's nothing quite like that tender, right-from-the-stalk-to-the-pot-to-the-table flavor of home-grown sweet corn.

In this chapter you'll find tips to plant, cultivate, and enjoy this favorite vegetable. You can also have fun with other types of corn. Popcorn is popular at ball games, in the movies, and on outings. You can easily grow some popcorn from the ground up. Ornamental corn also is fun to decorate your home in the fall and sell on your vegetable stand.

CORN HISTORY

Corn has been growing on the good planet Earth since far back in time. But corn, or maize, as it is called in some parts of the world, puzzles scientists even today. They can't seem to find its wild ancestors. Early explorers and settlers discovered corn in America. Indians grew it for a basic part of their diet. Ancient corn was discovered in a cave in New Mexico dating back 4,000 years. It really must be a long-established native of the Western Hemisphere, since, strangely enough, no word of corn is found in the Bible.

Corn is a large member of the grass family, called Graminae. It has fibrous wood stalks that may grow from a few feet to 25 feet tall. There are many types today, all tracing their heritage back to the original, multicolored Indian corn.

There are six principal types of corn. One of the earliest types still in use today is popcorn, which has a unique ability to explode when it is heated. Sweet corn is another type. Soft corn is also called flour corn because of its special use as flour. There is also flint corn and dent corn. These are the most widely grown for processing and livestock feed. As dent corn dries in the field each kernel develops a dent. There is also a pod corn, which is not grown today.

A full history of corn and its importance to mankind, especially to our American economy, would take a full book. For fun, read up on this most widely grown American crop. You'll be amazed how much this simple plant has meant to so many millions of people since it was first discovered by the early settlers.

THE USES OF CORN

The central states of these United States are often called the Corn Belt. Since our nation was first founded, corn has stood tall as one of the most important crops ever grown here. As many people realize, this nation is based on a corn economy. For a school project, you may wish to investigate and trace the many vital uses of corn.

Study the illustrations shown. Then look up corn in reference books in your library. There's much to find and learn. From just these little diagrams you can find food for thought and a school project as you dig into the fascinating field of corn.

CORNY FACTS OF LIFE

Corn has become one of the most widely grown, used, and valuable crops known to modern civilization. It bears your close attention, because it really is King Corn to millions.

Corn begins from the kernels, which are monocot-type seeds. As it sprouts, this seed sends down roots to fetch up water and nutrients. Soon it develops stem and leaves.

As it matures, you'll find many long leaves reaching out to catch the sun's energy-giving rays so that it may grow taller and produce its tassels and eventually its ears.

When fully grown, the corn plant is tipped by a spiked tassel. This part produces the male flowers of the plant. Down along the stalk other spikes form. These contain the female parts of the plant, growing out from the base of leaves. Some varieties have only one ear, others two or more. From a germ, or bud, on the spike, these ears grow filaments called silk.

When the pollen ripens on the tassels it blows down to the ends of the silks. This fertilizes the ears so that kernels develop. If you don't grow corn in several parallel rows, your ears may not fill out. That's because the pollen doesn't get to pollinate the ears. In the following pages you'll learn tricks to do with corn so that it grows tall and sweet and tasty for you as it has done for thousands of years for others.

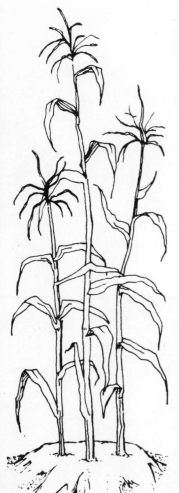

PLANTING CORN

"Corn, sweet corn, how lovely you grow for me. I love corn, as far as the eye can see. First you plant the seeds, then you pull the weeds, then stand back and watch your corn grow."

Those happy lines are from a song we heard sung recently in tribute to one of the most All-American of all home garden vegetables. Sweet corn may not be quite that easy to grow, but if you follow the directions given here, you'll be able to sing along with your tall and stately corn.

You should plant corn seeds as soon as your soil is warm and dry in the spring. Corn seeds, like beans, can rot if the ground is too wet and cold. Farmers advise planting corn right after the last full moon in May. Some do plant earlier, but if you want corn knee-high by the Fourth of July, you must plant early. You may plant rows or use the hill method. In rows, plant at least four parallel rows so pollen from tassels will pollinate the ears. Without pollination the ears won't be filled full of kernels.

Follow planting directions on the seed packet label. For hills, place several seeds in a circle. Space hills 2 to 3 feet apart. Be sure to add fertilizer halfway through the growing season, about July 4th, so your plants get a boost when they are growing most rapidly. Water well each week as the corn begins to tassel, so ears will form plump and full and as sugar sweet as possible.

INTERPLANTING CORN

Corn grows taller than most other crops in our home gardens. To keep it growing well, you must remove the weeds that grow between the rows. Here's a way to save yourself some work. Let other plants grow along the ground to act as a living mulch.

This process is called interplanting. Farmers use this to grow pumpkins on the same fields in which they have planted corn. It may not be as satisfactory as giving both plants the optimum light, fertilizer, and water, but it sure saves space.

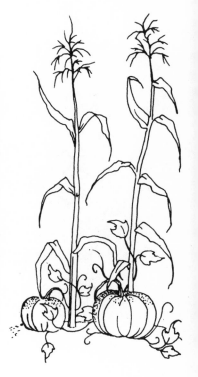

Plant your rows of corn. When they are started well, several inches high, cultivate carefully to eliminate weeds. Then, between several rows plant some hills of pumpkins. You can also plant cucumbers or other vine crops that crawl along the ground. As they spread, their vines will become covered with leaves. True, the sunlight doesn't penetrate to them as well as it should. True, too, you must feed and water both corn and those interplanted crops in the same area.

However, as the vines spread out, they'll shade the ground. This holds moisture in the soil and helps to stop a lot of pesky weeds from getting a strong roothold. Do weed periodically. Try this age-old idea. Two crops from one area is a proven, useful ground-saver.

INSECT ENEMIES

Sweet corn is enjoyed by hungry worms as well as by people. If you don't stop them they'll eat or damage your corn ears before you get to taste them.

The corn earworm, also known as the tomato fruitworm and bollworm, is one of the most common pests. Light brown moths lay tiny eggs which hatch into hungry larvae at the ear tips. They eat down the silks, entering the ear and eating the kernels. They may be light brown, cream, or even green in color. Damage is caused by their eating and the molds that may form.

The European corn borer attacks many crops, although corn is its favorite. Eggs are laid like fish scales in masses of 15 to 20 beneath corn leaves. Tiny borers hatch and crawl into protected spots. They feed on tissues of leaves and tassels. Soon they move down to bore into the stalks and ears. Since these pests must spend the winter in cornstalks, removing their home each fall helps to get rid of most of them.

White grubs, those soft, puffy, brown-headed larvae of May beetles, have lots of similar relatives. All do their damage by chewing off the tender roots of corn and other plants. Pearly white eggs are laid by the adult beetles in the soil. You can break the grub cycle by rotating crops from vegetables to green manure-grass. Soil treatment chemicals also have been useful, as farmers in the Corn Belt of America know.

The other corn pests can be most effectively stopped by careful pesticide applications. New, tight-husk hybrid varieties also resist some of these above-ground borers.

CORN VARIETIES

You can grow many varieties of sweet corn. The hybrid varieties are best because they have been developed to provide earlier harvest, faster growth, sweeter taste, and larger, better-filled ears. You can also grow some of the ornamental types and popcorn, too, if you wish. Try these top-rated varieties.

YELLOW CORN

Golden Cross Bantam is high quality. It grows well and is fine fresh, frozen, or canned. Most stalks bear two ears 7 to 8 inches long with 10 to 14 rows of light golden kernels per ear.

Illini Xtra Sweet matures in about 85 days. It is twice as sweet as others because its sugar content does not turn to starch as rapidly. You should get 2 or more ears per stalk. Ears are 8 inches long with 14 to 16 rows of tasty golden kernels.

Early Xtra Sweet is an All-America selection. It has outstanding sweetness and matures earlier than Illini. It has 12 to 16 rows of kernels on ears 7 to 9 inches long. This variety grows about 6 feet tall.

Honeycross is a top-quality wilt-resistant

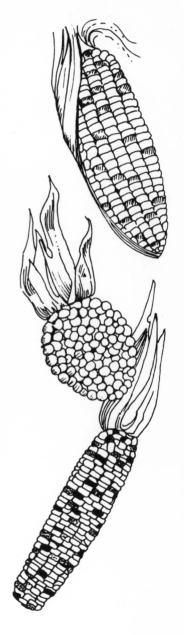

variety with 8- to 9-inch-long ears having 16-plus rows of bright yellow, deep kernels. It also resists ear worm and smut damage and does well in a variety of soil conditions.

WHITE CORN

If you like white corn, try Stowell's Evergreen Hybrid. It yields deep, uniform kernels on 7- to 8-inch-long ears with 14 to 18 rows per ear. Expect to pick in 90 days.

For early white corn, try Silver Sweet. It has small ears 6 inches long with 10 to 12 rows of extra-sweet kernels in about 65 days from the time you plant your seeds.

Country Gentleman Hybrid takes 90 days to mature, but has the flavor of old standard Country Gentleman with 7- to 8-inch ears and lots of tasty eating per ear.

YELLOW AND WHITE CORN

Honey and Cream is a new sweet corn now widely grown both in home gardens and commercially. It has contrasting bright white and yellow kernels on 7- to 8-inch ears with 12 to 14 rows of kernels per ear.

POPCORN

Peppy Popcorn Hybrid provides outstanding popability and taste. It matures in 90 days, bears 2 or more ears per stalk and produces nice, tender popcorn. Cream Puff Hybrid takes 100-plus days to mature, but yields well and tastes good, too.

ORNAMENTAL CORN

You can try Strawberry Ornamental popcorn. It is popable and decorative. Ears are only 2 inches long and almost 2 inches across. It matures in about 100 days.

Rainbow is primarily a showy corn, the so-called Indian corn. It has large ears with various shades of yellow, red, orange, and even blue. This is one to grow for table decorations and door displays for your holiday seasons.

CORN RECIPES

Nothing seems quite so tasty as mouth-watering corn on the cob, dripping with butter and lightly salted. But you can enjoy corn in other ways: creamed, made into relish, and in pudding. Good cookbooks have a number of fine recipes. Here are some we like.

CORN ON THE COB

New varieties have the ability to produce more sugar content in the kernels. The faster you get the corn from garden to boiling pot of water, the finer the taste will be. Corn left to stand in the hot sun after picking will lose quality. That's because the sugar turns into starch.

Pick corn just before you cook it. Husk it and remove the silks. Check for any pests that may have burrowed into the ear. Cut away any damaged parts.

Boil water rapidly. Drop the ears into the water, bring back to a rolling boil, and cook for no more than 3 minutes. Overcooking also destroys the sweetness. As soon as they are done, remove the ears from the water and serve topped with melted butter.

SUCCOTASH

Pick fresh corn, husk, and wash. Pick and shell tender lima beans. Put on two pots to boil. You can cook the corn on the cob and remove the kernels after cooking, or use a kernel remover to pop them off before cooking.

If you cook corn on the cob, undercook it a minute or so. Then add the kernels you remove from the cob to the other pot of boiling water, in which you will have put the lima beans to cook for about 7 to 10 minutes. They should be almost tender. Cook the corn and lima beans together for one minute, then pour off the water and serve. That special blend of tender beans and corn is a magic combination.

REDISCOVER
SQUASH

Squash has been a vegetable favored for centuries for many of its values: ease of growing, high yields, sweet taste, and keep-ability. As modern canning and freezing methods were developed, other vegetables gained in popularity, often because these developments enabled families to enjoy a wider range of foods in their year-round diets.

During the past few years, many people have returned to natural gardening. They have rediscovered that there is a delicious difference between fully ripe home-grown garden food and store-bought vegetables.

With this discovery has come a curiosity to try other types of vegetables. Squash, which had been somewhat neglected, is now being rediscovered. More folks are growing it not just for the many pleasing tastes of different varieties, but for its age-old virtues as well.

You can grow a few plants of different types of squash in small garden plots. Since one package of seeds will produce many plants and an abundance of squash, plan to swap seeds of your variety with friends. That way you'll have a few plants of each variety and you'll gain a tastier selection for your dining pleasure.

SQUASH HISTORY

When is a squash not a squash? When it really is a pumpkin or a gourd. Squashes, gourds, and pumpkins belong to a strange and puzzling family group. Gourds may look colorful but are inedible. Actually, most of the so-called squashes which we grow for food in our home gardens are pumpkins. If the stem is ridged and furrowed or flares at the point where it joins the fruit, it is a pumpkin. If it is soft, spongy and cylindrical, and is not enlarged at this junction, it is a squash.

Using this basic rule, many fruits you thought were squashes are really pumpkins, and vice versa. One major group of squash belongs to the genus *Cucurbita maxima*. These include the Hubbard, Sibley, and various turban types. The *Cucurbita pepo* family is actually a family of pumpkins. The summer squash, straight and crookneck Scallop, Patty Pan, and several others belong to the pumpkin family.

To complicate matters even more, the Cashews, Japanese crooknecks, and Sweet Potato squashes belong to another family, *Cucurbita moschata,* which, from the best records available, probably are originally native to Asia.

Whether you grow a pumpkin and call it a squash or a squash that is really a pumpkin, there is one thing all have in common. Properly grown, they will reward you with growing and eating fun.

INSECT ENEMIES

Squash bugs can really bug you and your squash. These pests, like most, seem suddenly to find their way to your garden. One day the plants are fine. The next week you'll see holes in leaves. A few days later these pests are busily sucking the life out of your squash leaves, vines, and fruit. Leaves can wilt rapidly. Small plants can be killed. Even mature plants may die.

The half-inch-long black bugs lay rounded clusters of reddish eggs. These hatch and young wingless nymphs emerge to suck plant's sap. There is usually only one hatch a year.

Pickleworms bother squash as well as cucumbers and melons. Brown moths with creamy wing markings lay eggs on plants, singly or in small clusters among flowers, leaf buds, young leaves, and fruit. They hatch in 3 days. Young pickleworms feed on the surface at first, then tunnel into vines, stems, and flowers.

The squash vine borer hatches from eggs laid by a clear-winged moth. Larvae grow rapidly, reaching maturity in 4 weeks. They tunnel into vines, causing them to wilt rapidly and die. These also attack other vine crops. There is usually one generation in northern gardens, perhaps two in southern regions.

Since the eggs and tiny larvae of these squash pests are difficult to find, most authorities recommend a careful application of pesticides whenever any signs of damage are found.

SQUASH VARIETIES

Here are some of the more outstanding squash varieties for your garden. Plant and pick your pleasure.

SUMMER SQUASH

Early Golden Summer Crookneck grows quickly. You can begin picking these meaty bright yellow squash in 50 days or so. They are delicious, have fine texture, and freeze well. Pick when 4 to 6 inches long.

Aristocrat Hybrid, a green zucchini-type with bush growth habit, matures in 48 days. These squash are smooth, cylindrical, and tasty.

Golden Zucchini ripens in 50 days and has a glossy, bright color to its slender, cylindrical fruits. It has a distinctive zucchini flavor.

St. Pat Scallop is an All-America winner. Early and vigorous, it yields bell-shaped fruit. Patty Pan is pale green with flat fruits changing to creamy white. Pick when 6 inches across.

FALL AND WINTER SQUASH

The flesh of butternut squash is orange-colored and fine-textured with a sweet, and nutty flavor. Fruits are about 8 to 10 inches long, buff-colored and with a smooth, hard shell.

True Hubbard is popular for late fall harvest and winter storage. Fruits mature dark bronze-green with deep, dry, yellow-orange flesh inside. Pick in about 115 days when mature. Blue Hubbard's shell is slightly ridged and blue-gray. The flesh is orange, fine-grained, tasty, and freezes well.

Buttercup, maturing in 105 days, has thick orange flesh that cooks sweetly. It has turban-shaped fruit, 4 to 7 inches across. The blossom end has a prominent button. This squash is dark green with white stripes. It also keeps well over winter.

Waltham Butternut matures early in 85 days, has delicious flavor, yields well, and keeps better. It is an All America winner for its many improved characteristics.

Turk's Turban is an ornamental squash maturing in 100 days. You get heavy yields of 8- to 10-inch bright orange-red flattened fruits with stripes of scarlet, orange, cream, white, and green. Good for table decorations.

Bush Table Queen or Acorn squash is named for its distinctive acorn shape. These green, deeply ribbed fruits mature 5 inches long, 4 inches wide on semibush plants. They bear well in little space. When the skin hardens it keeps well and protects the sweet orange flesh.

Royal Acorn is family-size, maturing 6 to 8 inches long and 6 inches across, with dark green color that turns dull orange in storage. This squash is finely flavored for cooking and baking.

SUPER-SIZE SQUASH

You can grow one variety of super-size squash that keeps getting bigger and bigger and bigger. Unfortunately it is not edible, but what an eye catcher it is.

If you have extra room around your home grounds try a hill of Right Royal squash. Burpee and other firms sell the seeds. You'll need an area about 10 to 12 feet, or bigger if possible, because this giant needs room to roam. Its vines sprawl far and wide.

Because of its gigantic vine and fruit size, it needs lots to eat and drink, too. Even without the special watering tricks discussed in this chapter, a Right Royal squash can grow from seed to 100, 200, 300 pounds or more in just one season.

To grow the biggest squash possible you should add a booster helping of 1 to 2 cups of fertilizer around the hill at least once during the growing season. Naturally, you should have prefertilized before or at the time you plant the seeds.

When you see the first blooms appear, save just a few. Pick the other flowers off when fruit has set at one or two points along each vine. Vines will then put their growing efforts into the few remaining fruits. If you have fed it well and given this unique squash enough water as it grows, you will most likely astound anyone who leans over your back fence for a peek. One word of caution. Don't try lifting it. You'll probably need some helping hands to move it.

The Right Royal isn't totally impractical, however. You can roll it to a prime location and decorate it for Halloween.

STORE YOUR SQUASH

Summer squash can be frozen or used in a variety of recipes all summer. Winter squash are even better because you can store them easily all winter and enjoy their bounty anytime you like.

Winter squash should be planted in late spring or early summer. That gives them time to mature to their full size. Unlike summer types that should be picked young and tender, winter squash varieties must be allowed to mature so their rinds are firm and hard. When they do, this protects them from decay, so long as they don't freeze.

Whichever winter squash you decide to grow, all enjoy the same general keeping conditions. Move them indoors just before the first killing frost of fall. You usually get a warning with a light frost that turns some leaves brown in spots. That's your signal.

Place your winter squash in a cool, not too dry location. A basement or garage that doesn't freeze is good. Keep them separated so that any damage to one doesn't start decay moving to others. If you keep them at 45 to 55 degrees, you will be able to store winter squash like Hubbard and its hard-rinded relatives for weeks and months. They'll be sitting pretty there, awaiting your decision to cut them up and cook them into a variety of tasty dishes. Pumpkins, too, can be stored in the same cool rooms as winter squash.

SQUASH-GROWING FUN

Squash, like most vegetables, is composed primarily of water. The plants become especially thirsty when they begin to flower and set fruit. You must devotedly supply their large moisture needs at this critical period, otherwise you won't get either the quantity or quality you want.

Here's a good growing idea borrowed from some of our champion squash gardeners. They place several quart or gallon jars in the ground around their squash plant hills. Then, they keep them filled with water and lead a fiberglass wick, frayed at each end, from the jar into the soil in the hill. They even add a slurry or mixture of cow manure or fertilizer to the water. The wick transfers this nutrient solution into the soil where the growing roots can take it up to stimulate their faster growth.

You can use liquid seaweed or other organic plant foods, such as manures, but there might be a smell. Chemical fertilizer mixed with one tablespoon of 5-10-5 per gallon works just as well, they say. The giant squash you can grow with this method will make you the envy of your neighborhood.

Another simple yet effective way to boost growth of squash and any other plants you grow in hills puts compost to work in an out-of-the-way place . . . right in the garden.

Dig several holes. Fill these holes with leaves and other organic matter. Throw in a few spadesful of manure. Add more leaves and old grass clippings. As this organic matter decays it forms a steadily released supply of plant food. Then, plant your squash around this compost pit. Or plant tomatoes or pole beans or corn. Your compost-making pit is out of sight but being used to advantage to improve garden soil and nourish your plants.

TASTY SQUASH TREATS

SAUTEED ZUCCHINI

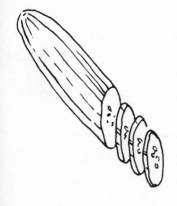

Wash young zucchini, preferably no longer than 6 inches each. Cut them into thin slices, crosswise. Heat butter or oil in a frying pan. Add the zucchini and sauté it slowly until it is tender. Be sure to turn the slices often. Season the squash with salt and pepper, sweet basil, or marjoram. If you like, you can add garlic or grated onion to the oil. The zucchini may be served with grated cheese; sour cream and chopped parsley or chives; or a nice tomato sauce.

FRIED ZUCCHINI AND PEPPERS WITH TOMATOES

1 pound zucchini, each about 6 inches long
3 medium-size green peppers
¼ cup oil
1 teaspoon salt
1 cup diced tomatoes
¼ teaspoon oregano, or to taste
⅛ teaspoon black papper

Scrub squash and green peppers and slice them into strips, about 2 inches long and about ½ inch wide. Heat the oil in a heavy frying pan and add the squash and pepper strips. Cook until they are just lightly browned. Add the tomatoes and salt and simmer together until the vegetables are soft, about 12 minutes. Season with the oregano and black pepper. Yield: 5 servings.

PROJECTS, CONTESTS, THINGS TO DO

YOUNG AMERICA GARDENING CONTEST

As you perfect your good growing skills, you can have a fine chance to win awards. Aim high. Enter one of the Young America Horticulture Contests. They are sponsored by the National Junior Horticultural Association and are open to anyone 17 years of age or under.

These annual contests let you test your gardening skills against thousands of other young gardeners like yourself. There is no cost to participate. The contests offer you a chance to demonstrate your skill at growing things. You can compete in four possible contests. One is gardening. Another is plant propagation. The third one is called environmental beautification, and the fourth is experimental horticulture.

There are contests in four age groups, from 8 years old and younger through 15 to 17 years old. There are contests for older youths and young adults, too.

Awards include certificates and gifts. Judging is based on the reports submitted by contestants.

One recent winner, a 12-year-old from Tiger, Georgia, grew an acre of green snap beans for his project. It earned him over $300. Another winner propagated a wide variety of plants, from African violets to canna lilies.

The address for more information is National Junior Horticultural Association, 384 Colonial Avenue, Worthington, Ohio 43085.

WIN PRIZES

Growing flowers is lots of fun. You can enjoy them outdoors or indoors as cut flower displays in many ways. Once you learn how to grow flowers well, try your luck at winning some prizes in local flower shows. There are shows in almost every town that often accept entries from amateurs. You might even join a 4-H Gardening Club to expand your knowledge of good gardening. To win prizes, read the entry form of the show carefully. When the entry form specifies one or two or three or five blooms, that's all you should display. Pick the best, most typical blooms of that particular variety. They should be uniform, free from damage, and in their prime of life. Avoid mismatching sizes unless, of course, you are entering a mixed arrangement class. Cut some extra blooms to take with you, so if one is damaged on the way you have an alternate bloom in its place. In most shows, simple containers are best. Some shows provide them. Keep in mind that you want to display your blooms, not the container. Take time to arrange flowers so they all show to advantage and are not crowded. You may not win top prize at first, but keep on trying. As you improve your growing skills, that beautiful blue-ribbon day will surely arrive.

SHOW AND TELL

Try a root-watcher's box to learn more about how plants grow. All you need is some boards, screws or nails, a clear-plastic viewing side, and soil in which to plant your seeds.

Cut three boards of 1 x 4 inch wood, each 12 inches long. Attach both sides to the bottom piece. Then cut a piece of plywood to fit the back. Finally, cut a piece of clear-plastic sheet to cover the front. When all pieces are fastened tightly, putty the seams so the box won't leak. Then fill it with soil and plant your seeds. Any seeds will do, but radish and corn sprout more quickly and roots form faster. Water every few days. Then describe how fast the seeds sprout and how roots form as you watch nature's underground mysteries unfold.

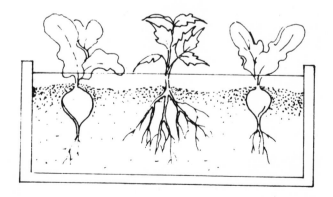

SCIENCE FAIR

You have probably heard about soil erosion.
That's the washing away of soil in the rain,
especially on steep slopes that have no plant
growth to hold soil in place. You can make a
soil-erosion demonstration board to prove
why crops should be planted across slopes to
prevent erosion. Cut a piece of plywood 2 x
4 feet. Attach sides of 1 x 3 inch wood. Fill
the box you make with soil. Then raise one
side 12 inches higher than the other. You
can easily show erosion in action on unprotected soil by sprinkling water from a
watering can on the upper area. Watch how
gullies form as erosion begins. Then describe your observations in a report for
class, perhaps for extra credit, or a Science
Fair project.

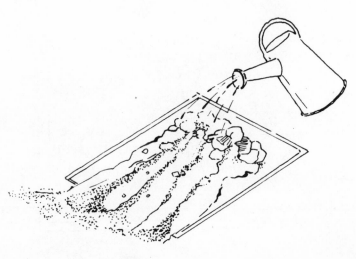

DECORATE WITH BLOOMS

Flowers look lovely in the garden, but half the reason for growing them is to enjoy them indoors, too. Here are tips to help you brighten your home with blooming bouquets.

Select the colors that will harmonize with the wallpaper or color of the paint on walls. You might wish to pick the flower colors to accent draperies or a piece of furniture, or to emphasize a certain color in rugs and carpets. Then, cut your blooms just as they are opening. That way they will last a longer time indoors as cut flowers. Cut the best blooms cleanly with scissors. You can mix and match with different varieties or even by using different types of flowers. Then remove the leaves from the lower stems. Otherwise they will hasten decay and perhaps cause an odor. Place the flowers in any type of container, such as a vase, glass, or pitcher, and let them bush out. Then, cut some stems shorter to create a rounded, full appearance. You can coax the bouquet into more interesting shapes and lines. Experiment a bit. Decide how the blooms look best to you.

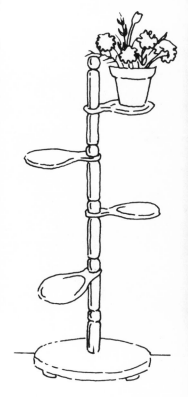

You can also obtain handy flower-arranging foam-filled vases from florists, or cut pieces of styrofoam to the size of the base of your container. Then, you simply insert the pointed ends of the stems into the base to hold your blooms in the most pleasing arrangement.

Use warm water when you make flower arrangements. Warm water flows up the cut stems faster and better to keep the blooms fresh longer. There are also special preparations you can mix and apply to prolong the life of your cut blossoms. Remember, the more you cut, the more your blooms will grow.

DECORATE CONTAINERS

Never say you don't have some way to grow flowers around your home. Look around. There are probably all sorts of containers available, though they may not look like much now. It is up to you to change that. With a bit of imagination and some colorful cloth, burlap, or paint, you can really create eye-appealing and useful decorative containers for plants. Save large coffee or soup cans or other tubs, and buckets, too. Plastic pails and old baskets are fine.

All you need to do is line any very leaky container with heavy plastic trash bags to hold the soil mix. Of course, you must provide for proper drainage. A few holes in the bottom will do. Next, find old cloth that can be dyed. Attach burlap or dyed cloth around the container neatly. Pin on special designs, if you like. On some containers just a bright coat of paint may be all it takes. Add some floral decals and you'll have converted those unsightly, useless containers into handy, decorative planters for flowers and potted mini-vegetables.

Be creative. Turn your imagination loose. Explore the cellar, attic, garage, and closets.

Then set to work to give those tubs, pots, and baskets new uses as colorfully decorative flower planters.

TRY A WINDOW BOX

If you don't have a yard in which to garden, you can still enjoy your flowers in a window box. It's easy to make one. Fun, too. Measure your window. Then cut three boards the same length as your window is wide. Next cut the two shorter side pieces. Assemble the box with screws to be sure it holds together well. Drill holes in the bottom to let excess water and rain escape. Then mount it outside under your window with strong metal brackets. Finally, put your potted flowers right into it, or fill it with soil and start your garden from seeds. Blooming fun is anywhere you can grow some plants to please yourself and add flower power to your life.

GROW A LIVING FLAG

To welcome America's Bicentennial, many gardeners planted red, white, and blue flowers as a patriotic gesture. Some were perennial plantings from tulip and hyacinth bulbs. They were shaped like Colonial American flags or bunting streamers. Other gardeners grew their living flags in the form of annual flowers, such as red, white, and blue asters. These delightful, beautiful living flags led other gardeners to design and plan colorful flags from their family's heritage, honoring the countries from which their forefathers had come.

You, too, can pick a flag, and plant and grow it, perhaps as a community beautification project in cooperation with a local or area garden club. Here's how to design and grow a living flag: Check an encyclopedia's section on flags to find many full-color pictures. Pick a sunny spot, about 6 x 10 feet. Plot the flag on paper first. That way you will know exactly in which rows the red, white, and blue plants should grow to give the colorful design of your flag. Be sure to select flowers that grow about the same height. Otherwise, the taller ones will overshadow the low ones.

Prepare the ground well. Mark the rows. Use lime to mark circles or other special designs on the ground so that the plants may be set right where they should be. Then begin to plant your seeds or seedlings. Weeds can sneak in before plants can set firm roots, so cultivate between rows, or

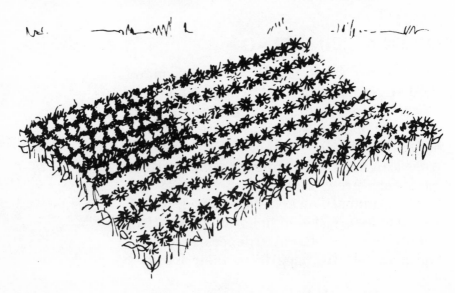

mulch. Mulching is better. By using wood chips or peat moss, you save soil moisture, smother weeds, and obtain a nice ground color that sets off your overall design attractively.

Some flags are simple—just three bands or stripes, horizontally or vertically, like the Swedish, French, or Italian flags. Pick the one you like, select matching-color flowers, and grow a lovely living flag.

ENJOY FLOWERING HANGUPS

Many low-growing flowers and vegetables are excellent for use in hanging baskets around your patio or porch. They need little care to reward you well. You can select almost any type of container, from clay pot to wooden basket or tub. Decorative ceramic planters or special pots with built-on saucers work well, too. Just pick a sunny spot. Use decorative chain, woven plastic, or fancy macrame ropes to hold the containers. You can make hangers yourself just by looping a cord around the pot and attaching other cords to support it from a rafter, hook, or bracket. Perhaps at summer camp or in crafts classes at school you can make some hangers as gifts.

Remember the golden growing rule for any potted plants like these: No plants like wet feet. Always put gravel in the bottom of any container so roots don't rest in excess water. It is important, too, that drainage be provided. But if you hang the plants, be sure they don't drip on furniture and stain it. Double potting works well for these hanging plants.

143

TRY A ROADSIDE STAND

Once your vegetables ripen and your flowers blossom, you may have more than your own family needs. You'll want to share some with friends. You still may have extras. Think about selling them at your own roadside stand. Many people want nice fresh vegetables and beautiful bouquets. The money you earn can pay for next year's seed and fertilizer, and give you spending money, besides. Ask your parents about the idea. All you need is a small table plus a sign. Display your crops and flowers neatly. Keep cut flowers shaded so they won't wilt. Letter the sign carefully. Have paper bags so customers can carry their purchases home easily. Check local stores to learn what vegetables are worth. Home-grown produce has a freshly picked taste and is usually worth more. Try your hand at a roadside stand. It's a fun way to profit from your garden.

TRY A ROUTE

When you garden, you'll most likely have more flowers and vegetables than you can use at once. Some you can sell on your roadside stand. If you also have grown vegetables in their own garden or mixed among your flowers, how about a flower and vegetable route to sell your surplus? First, discuss the idea with your parents and get their permission. Then, ask neighbors and relatives what they would like to buy each week. Make a list. Then, once a week, pick plump, ripe vegetables and beautiful blooms. Wash the vegetables well. Put them in a basket along with bouquets of blooms. You want your samples to look their best so that you'll get repeat orders week after week. Tell your customers that you grow the plants yourself and will deliver them every week. You'll be surprised how many people will welcome you.

TRY DRYING FLOWERS

Once you have grown beautiful, full blooms on your flower plants, you can cut them for bouquets or table arrangements. Sooner or later these blooms will fade and die. Now, there is a simple and relatively easy way to preserve flowers so that you can enjoy them for months and even years to come. Try drying them. Drying the flower blooms requires some patience and practice, but it is rewarding. The best way is to buy a

prepared kit called Flower Dri. It includes
1½ pounds of silica gel drying material plus
many feet of floral tape, wire, and a special
step-by-step booklet. Silica gel is a material
that absorbs moisture quickly. It is harm-
less, easy to use, and inexpensive. This gel
removes moisture from flowers so quickly
they don't shrivel or loose their color.

Pick the flowers—the most perfect blooms
around—on a dry day. Remove the foliage
and cut the stems 2 inches long. Place the
flowers upside down in a container, then
sprinkle to cover with the silica gel. Cover
well and then seal the container tightly. Put
it away for a week. Then open it carefully,
pour off the top gel, and remove the flowers.
Blow the last particles off and you'll have a
beautifully dried specimen to use in your
own arrangements for months.

ROCK GARDENS ARE LOVELY

If you have a sloping, sunny spot, consider
the value of a rock garden. Once you plant
that area with perennials and mulch it well,
the plants will take root and spread. Their

roots will hold the soil. The rocks will provide an attractive, natural look. After a year or two, you'll have little work to do except remove the few weeds that invade the area. With a touch of fertilizer each season, rock gardens will reward you with permanent beauty for years to come.

Rocks are available everywhere. Selecting the right ones can be fun. When you travel, go on a picnic, or see new home foundations being dug, you'll have ample opportunity to pick and choose the rocks you want. You may decide to have them all similar, such as those sturdy stones and rocks along roadsides in your area. Sometimes, flat or unusually shaped rocks will serve your purpose.

You can also begin a rock collection. In your travels with your family, keep an eye peeled for specimens. Some may have attractive lines or odd shapes. Others may have minerals streaking them in lovely and striking patterns. All you have to do is collect a few each trip afield. Then, dig them into your soil. Plant your flowers, ivy, and other plants around them and bit by bit your rock garden will come alive.

PLAN YOUR GARDEN

Advance planning will help guide you to growing success. Use these graph pages to map out your garden. One square equals 12 inches. Tomatoes, for example, need 3 to 4 feet between plants. If you grow them on hoops or stakes, plant 3 feet apart. Three

tomato plants will provide enough tomatoes for each person in your family. As you map out where other vegetables should go, consult the chart on the next page. It gives proper spacing of the most popular, easily grown vegetables.

VEGETABLE PLANTING GUIDE

Here are the best spacings for the most popular vegetables. As you plan your garden, use these figures to map out where each one will be so that they all have proper room to grow well.

Plant	Seed Depth	Space Between Rows	Distance Within Rows
Beans, Bush	1″	2-3 ft	3-4″
Beans, Pole	1-1½″	2 ft	3 ft
Beets	½″	15-18″	2-3″
Broccoli	¼″	3 ft	14-20″
Cabbage	½″	2 ft	14-20″
Carrots	¼″	1½-2 ft	2-3″
Cauliflower	½″	2 ft	14-20″
Corn, Sweet	1½″	3 ft	8-12″ rows, 2′ between hills
Cucumbers	½″	6 ft	3 x 3 ft rows, 6-ft hills
Eggplants	¼″	3-4 ft	2 ft
Lettuce, Head	1″	12-14″	10-14″
Lettuce, Leaf	½″	6″	6″
Muskmelons	1″	6″	6 x 6 ft hills
Onions, Sets	½″	12-14″	2-3″
Peas	1½″	2-3 ft	2″
Peppers	¼″	3 ft	14-20″
Pumpkins	1″	8-10 ft	3-4 ft
Radishes	¼″	1-2 ft	1″
Spinach	½″	12-14″	3-4″

Plant	Seed Depth	Space Between Rows	Distance Within Rows
Squash, Bush	1″	4 ft	4-ft hills
Squash, Vine	1-2″	8 ft	18-36″
Tomatoes	½″	2 ft	3-4 ft
Turnips	½″	14-18″	4-8″
Watermelons	1-2″	8 ft	8 ft

GARDEN RECORD

Good gardening begins by planning and keeping simple records. That way you know when to plant, fertilize, weed, feed, and pick what you have grown. To make gardening easier this year and next, just fill in the facts you want to remember. Then you can easily refer to your book to improve your growing ability year after year.

Here's a useful list you can follow. Of course, you can add more information right on this page as you watch your plants grow.

My flower garden is _____ feet by _____ feet. I started seeds indoors on _____ , after the last spring frost, which came on _____. I began improving the soil on _____ and fertilized my garden with _____ on _____, using (number of cups or pounds) _____. I watered my garden _____ times, beginning on _____. My first flower was a _____ and was ready to pick on _____. The last flower I picked was a _____ on _____, before first frost, which arrived on

_____. My biggest flower was a _____. It measured _____ inches across. My tallest flower was a _____. To grow better flowers next year I should begin my indoor seeds on _____ and begin transplanting and seeding outdoors on _____. The frost-free date in my area usually is _____. Next year the most important changes to make in my flower garden are: _____.

_____
_____ .

GARDEN
GLOSSARY

Many gardening words have special meanings, which you should learn in order to become a better gardener.

Aerobic means the type of useful bacteria that must have air in which to work best to break down leaves, manure, and other organic materials into compost or humus.

All-America is a term that describes flowers or vegetables that grow well under strict test-growing conditions in many parts of our country. When a new flower or vegetable grows better than has any previous variety, it may win a gold, silver, or bronze medal and be named an *All-America* selection. Its seeds may cost more, but the results are worth it. They grow, bloom, and bear well.

Anaerobic means those helpful soil bacteria that can digest all types of organic material without air. These bacteria do their work more slowly than the aerobic types of soil bacteria.

Annual means a plant that grows from seed one year and is killed by frost. *Annuals* (unless they are hybrids) usually bloom and produce seeds which you can save to plant next year.

Blooms are flowers and are also called blossoms.

Carnation-flowered means marigold blooms that resemble the flowers of typical carnations.

Chrysanthemum-flowered means blooms that look like mums.

Clay-type soils are those which have very small particles of soil. Because there is little air space between these tiny particles, air and plant roots can't penetrate as they must do to let plants grow well. These soils remain wet or soggy, which is harmful to plant roots.

Compost is loose, decayed, or rotted organic material that helps improve your garden soil.

Disease-resistant means that a certain variety of plant has been produced that is able to grow well and usually will not catch certain common diseases that would harm or kill a similar variety that does not have that extra immunity.

Fertilizer is any type of organic material or chemical compound which is used in a garden as plant food.

Fluorescent means the type of long tube light specially made to give plants the closest-to-natural rays that duplicate the sun's own rays.

Fruit set is the formation of vegetable or fruit from the pollinated flowers of your vegetable plants.

Germination means a seed's ability to sprout. Most seed packets give a germination guarantee because seeds are packed fresh every year and will grow if you plant them correctly.

Humus is the material produced from organic matter which rots down in compost piles.

Hybrids are plants produced by crossing two different but related types. The plants that grow from their seed usually display the best properties of each parent; are hardier, stronger, and more disease-resistant; and bloom or bear more abundantly than the parents.

Insecticide is any chemical used to kill insects.

Interplanting means planting an extra crop, such as cucumbers, between or among hills or rows of another plant.

Microorganisms are unseen living organisms that exist in the soil.

Mulch means any material such as grass clippings, leaves, straw, or compost that has been living and will slowly decay to help improve your garden's soil. Other mulches, such as black plastic, also smother weeds and hold moisture in the soil, but do not help build better soil.

Nutrients are plant foods, usually the three basic elements of nitrogen, phophorus, and potash, needed for balanced plant growth.

Perennials are plants that grow from seed which become firmly established in your garden and regrow from roots year after year without planting new seed the following year. Seed packets tell you if a flower is annual or perennial.

Pesticide means a chemical used to control plant diseases as well as kill insects.

Roothold means outward growth of secondary roots from the first roots.

Rotary tilling means turning the soil with a machine so that soil on top is turned under, and clumps of sod and soil are churned into better condition for seed germination.

Soluble tape is a tape in which seeds are embedded or placed at equal distances and which dissolves when water touches it. The seeds are set free to sprout.

Styrofoam is a type of light, fluffy plastic used mainly for insulating. It is also useful for arranging blooms because it holds flowers in position when you poke stems into it.

Succession means planting new seeds or plants whenever you pick mature vegetables.

Thinning means removing weak or small seedlings.

Transplants are seedlings that have sprouted from seeds, and are ready to be moved to your outdoor garden.

Variety means related members of one plant family that all look somewhat alike. Varieties have their own names so that you can identify them, such as Fluffy Ruffles, Lilliput, or Cherry Buttons. Most seed companies pick a variety name that describes the color or the type of bloom or something else about that particular variety.

Vertical gardening means growing or training plants to grow up fences or poles. Growing up, not out, saves garden space.

INDEX

varieties, 117-19
corn borer, 116
cornflowers, 26
cosmos, 26
cucumbers, 12, 14, 88-96, 115, 124, 150
   history of, 89-90
   recipes with, 95
   varieties, 90, 91, 93, 94
cutworms, 14

day lily, 27
delphinium, 27
dianthus, 27, 28
dill, 65
downy woodpecker, 20
Dura test, 22
Dyro Lite Plant Lite, 21

eggplant, 150
endosperm, 4
English daisy, 28

fern, 28
fertilizers, 8, 14, 15, 16, 129, 156
flower arrangements, 139, 140, 144
Flower Dri, 146
flower fragrances, 29, 41
flowers, dried, 145, 146
fluorescent tubes, 21, 156
flycatchers, 20
forget-me-not, 27, 28
4-H Gardening Club, 136
four o'clocks, 26
foxglove, 28
frost, 25, 54, 62, 85, 98, 128
fruit set, 156
fungicides, 92

garden, pyramid, 10, 11
gardening, apartment, 21, 42, 48, 82, 107, 108, 141
gardening contests, 135-37
gardening glossary, 153-59
gardening records, 151-59
gardening sites, 6, 7, 21, 28, 34, 65, 80

lima beans, 120, 121
linum, 27
lobelia, 28
lupine, 26, 27

marigolds, 28, 31, 36–41, 75, 107
   history of, 37, 38
   varieties, 37, 39
melons, 124, 150
microorganisms, 157
mildew, 92
mint, 64
mock orange, 29
mosaic disease, 92
mosquitoes, 20
moss, 124
mulch, 15, 17, 76, 94, 115, 143, 146, 157

nasturtiums, 28
National Junior Horticulture Association, 135, 136
nematodes, 40
nicotiana, 126, 129
nitrogen, 16
nuthatches, 20
nutrients, 157
nymphs, 73

onions, 78, 86, 87, 150
overwatering, 5

pansies, 26, 28, 75, 107
parsley, 65, 87
peat moss, 5, 9, 84, 100, 143
peat trays, 5
peony, 29
peppers, 131, 150
pesticides, 19, 20, 40, 84, 100, 117, 157, 158
petunias, 25, 26, 28, 29, 54–59, 107
   history of, 55
   varieties, 56–58
phlox, 26, 28, 29
phosphorous, 16
photosynthesis, 16
pickles, 88–96

vermiculite, 5, 84
vertical gardening, 159
vinca, 26, 28
vines, 90, 93, 106, 115, 124, 127
violas, 26, 27, 28
violets, 28

wall flower, 29
wasps, 20
water content, 17
watering, 17
watermelons, 151
weeds, 15, 16, 80, 115, 142
weevils, 22
wilt, 92
window boxes, 28, 42, 69, 74
wisteria, 29
worms, 18, 19, 40, 73, 74, 83, 84, 92, 116, 118
wrens, 20

Young America Horticulture Contest, 135

zinnias, 26, 28, 31, 42-47, 107
  history of, 43
  varieties, 42-47
zucchini, 125, 130, 131

YOUR
GARDEN
NOTES